# LOSING IT

# LOSING IT

## A LIFETIME IN PURSUIT OF SPORTING EXCELLENCE

## SIMON BARNES

B L O O M S B U R Y
LONDON · OXFORD · NEW YORK · NEW DELHI · SYDNEY

Bloomsbury Sport
An imprint of Bloomsbury Publishing Plc

50 Bedford Square
London
WC1B 3DP
UK

1385 Broadway
New York
NY 10018
USA

www.bloomsbury.com

BLOOMSBURY and the Diana logo are trademarks of
Bloomsbury Publishing Plc

First published 2016

British Library Cataloguing-in-Publication Data
A catalogue record for this book is available from the British Library.

ISBN: HB: 978-1-4729-1877-2
ePub: 978-1-4729-1879-6

2 4 6 8 10 9 7 5 3 1

Typeset in Minion by Deanta Global Publishing Services, Chennai, India
Printed and bound in Great Britain by CPI Group (UK) Ltd, Croydon CR0 4YY

To find out more about our authors and books visit www.bloomsbury.com.
Here you will find extracts, author interviews, details of forthcoming
events and the option to sign up for our newsletters.

This is for all those I competed with, especially Roob and Salty. It's also for all those I competed against, especially the few that I (and we) managed to beat.

# Contents

**Part One: Protostar**

**A Star is Born**

**Part Three: Red Dwarf**
**A Star in Decay**

# Part One

# Protostar

---

## A Star is Born

# Chapter 1

# The Great Cricketer

Most people go into sports journalism because they failed at sport. So it's said, anyway. Not me. I went into sports journalism because I failed at writing. I've written lots of books and covered lots of great sport for newspapers – but that doesn't mean I haven't failed. I have failed to be James Joyce, I have failed to be Basho, I have failed to be Marcel Proust, I have failed to be Gerard Manley Hopkins, I have failed to be Anthony Powell, I have failed to be Ian Fleming. But the fact that I have failed as a writer doesn't mean I haven't failed at sport as well; it's just that sport wasn't the failure that propelled me into sports writing. All the same, my experiences of actually *doing* sport and mostly – not always – failing at it have informed my writing and understanding about sport: how could they not? And about life, yes, that too.

I have practised the trade of sportswriter since 1976, with the odd interruption. I have covered Redhill FC, seven summer Olympic Games, 20-odd Wimbledons, Super Bowls, World Cups, World Series; I've filled several passports with stamps and a lot of spiral-bound notebooks with frenzied italic scrawl, I was chief sportswriter at *The Times* for a dozen years. And everything I wrote about sport was informed, at some level, by the experience of doing it: by trying, by failing, by sometimes succeeding, by hoping too much and by caring too much. Experiences I have had on school playing fields, on village greens and at local shows are as vivid to me as my memories of Usain Bolt boogying to a world record in Beijing at the Olympic Games of 2008 or Australia reduced to two runs for three wickets in the first minutes of the Adelaide Test of 2010.

So let's start with a traumatic scene from childhood. After all, there are plenty of examples to imitate here. In *A la recherche du temps perdu*, it's the moment when the narrator's father abnegates. He gives up; the firm disciplinarian and hater of sentimentality offers the tearful Marcel his mother for the whole night – 'I don't want anything,' he explains unambiguously. And so the hell of being deprived of his mother's goodnight kiss is transformed into the highest heaven he is capable of imagining. In *A Portrait of the Artist as a Young Man* Stephen is unjustly beaten after his glasses were broken, so he dares to ask the rector, Father Conmee, to redress this terrible wrong. In the first volume of Anthony Powell's *A Dance to the Music of Time* Widmerpool, in his running gear, makes his ominous appearance, materialising out of the mist in preparation for haunting the 12 volumes of the work. What can I do but offer you a scene of comparable depth and power? So here is the story of the day I realised I wasn't a cricketer.

I was, I think, nine at the time, so I really ought to have had a realistic notion of my sporting capabilities. I had played cricket forever: played with my father in the garden and on Streatham Common with John Murtagh and others. I knew that it was never me that hit the ball across Streatham Common South into The Rookery ornamental gardens. I see now that I should have realised that I was a trifle short on natural talent. For some reason I didn't think that would matter when it came to proper organised cricket with an umpire.

It was here that I betrayed the fact that, for me, sport was a province that lay within the kingdom of the imagination. Sport was about gorgeous myths peopled with heroes, an endless unwinding narrative of glorious deeds. I had no idea of practical purpose, attainable goals and making the best of whatever abilities you happen to have. More real to me was the notion of kicking the ball against the garage door. I have to hit the target in order to save the world and bang! Did you guess right? Yes, the world was saved and I was the hero once again. This, surely, was the heart and meaning of sport.

But cricket always mattered far more. I knew more about cricket than anyone else at Sunnyhill Junior School: naturally I should have been the star cricketer. When we went to Birmingham to stay with the grandparents, my grandfather and I would catch the bus to Edgbaston and watch cricket – proper county cricket – all day with immense concentration. I would watch Norman Horner and Billy Ibadulla open the batting for Warwickshire, Big Jim Stewart came in at first drop, and then, with joy not unmixed with trepidation, I would watch the great M. J. K. Smith walk out to the crease, sometimes to score many runs, sometimes, paining me deeply, to fail. I would watch the Test matches on television; my mother used to keep a scorecard in her borderline-legible Bironic loops, updated with the fall of each wicket. I would read the cricket reports in the newspaper in the certainty that doing so made me an insider. A true believer. Cricket was a special thing to me. No one else at Sunnyhill understood cricket as I did, they didn't know the stuff about cricket that I did and the great names I could recite held no meaning for them. I *was* cricket: no one else in the school could claim such a thing. It was obvious, then, that I would play cricket better than anyone else.

Mr Gray took the cricket. He was a fine teacher, who also did the school play and ran the chess club after school on Monday evenings. In our third year, instead of playing rounders with the girls in the playground with a big round bat and a soft ball, we boys went out to play cricket on the school field with a straight cricket bat and a ball that hurt. It was a coming of age. Though I should point out that I had never showed any great proficiency even at rounders. I was a bit of a duffer, truth to tell, undersized and without any conspicuous natural gift of coordination. I knew all that, but I was also deeply certain of something else. I believed – I *knew* – that soon all this underachievement would be forgotten as if it had never been. Rounders, after all, was only rounders, but this was cricket – real, proper cricket with six-ball overs, a waving arm to indicate a four and a lifted index finger to signal the little death of dismissal. The wicket was matting, the stumps bail-less and driven into the ground as firmly as if they had been concreted. They were full-size: I can remember my astonishment at seeing these triple columns that reached almost to my armpits. The hard ball was nothing new to me. We wore pads to indicate the seriousness of the occasion: one pad for each batsman, worn on the leading leg, the one that takes most of the blows. When my turn came I strapped my pad on to my right leg with an air of calm certainty. Mr Gray had organised us into teams: Mrs Holland's class – my lot – against Mr Gray's. 3H vs 3G. Bring it on.

So picture me striding out to bat, in my shorts, single pad aflap. It was when I took guard that I realised my pad was on the wrong leg: it's the left leg that leads for a right-hander. But despite this dreadful solecism, I prepared to face the bowling.

What happened next perplexed me utterly. For nothing really happened.

The ball came and I was unable to do anything about it. I was frozen, not in terror, but in disbelief. The glorious transfiguration had failed to take place. I walked out as a weedy incompetent; I walked back unchanged. I could neither attack nor defend. I wasn't frightened of the ball or the bowler. I wasn't bowed down by responsibility or expectation. I just wasn't the person I thought I was. I just wasn't any good. I couldn't play. I really wasn't a cricketer after all.

I had thought it would just come to me. I thought that the moment I began to play proper grown-up cricket, my innate cover drive would at last leap free, unbound, in a glorious detonation of blessedness. I honestly thought that I would find myself playing a square cut, or rocking back to pull the ball to the boundary, leg-side, the man's side, as MJK called it. I thought that the act of playing proper cricket at last would see me emerging from a chrysalis: that I would spread my sporting wings and fly in brilliant colours across the grass of Sunnyhill playing fields. And I didn't.

It was my first real lesson about sport. I learned that there is no fantasy so outrageous that sport cannot encompass it. I learned that there is no sport without daydreams of greatness, and also that there is no sport without cruelty. I learned that sport only seems to be romantic: at the workplace it's about brutal and uncompromising practicalities. I also learned that sport is only truly cruel to those who truly care.

A bit like love.

# Chapter 2

# Bloody Cricket

'Do you want a game of bloody cricket?'

It was in this fashion – at least in the memory of John Murtagh – that I initiated our friendship. We were both ten at the time. He didn't think he was going to like me, finding such strong language repelling. My own memory is different: surely I was fairly deep into my teens before I started using words as powerful as 'bloody'. But no matter. John mixed an easy-going nature with a deep love of sport, and within minutes we were crossing Streatham Common North – possibly with adult supervision, for this was even then a busy road – to push the stumps into the receiving earth of Streatham Common itself. And so it began.

It was the first of a million games. John and I lived in the same terrace of six pebble-dashed houses set back a little from Hill House Road. He was number 1 The Terrace, I was number 4. The common was only a decent cricket hit away from The Terrace; even one of my cricket hits might have got there on a good day. We played bloody cricket all bloody summer, bashing the stumps into the ground with the bat handle, and after that we played bloody football all bloody winter, making a goal with jerseys in the classic fashion. Sometimes John's brother Matthew came to join us, sometimes our neighbour Roger. But mostly it was just us: batting and bowling, shooting and saving. You're out: my turn to bat. Three goals and in. What mattered was the rhythm of the game: you shoot, you score, you dive, you save, and then you change places. And on and on and on: across the vast eternities of childhood.

Here's the heart of the matter. John was better than me at batting, better than me at bowling, better than me at shooting, better than me at shot-stopping – even if I could actually give him a game there – *but it didn't matter*. I never felt any sense of humiliation; I don't think he felt a sense of superiority. It wasn't an unequal friendship: I wasn't despised because I couldn't hit a ball into The Rookery. It was just the way things were: we both wanted to play, and so we did.

Without me there was no game, there's that, of course. John needed me to beat if he was going to play, just as I needed someone to lose to. Not that it was really about winning and losing. We never totted these things up. We just played. It was no sport at all, or perhaps the purest form of sport, in which all the pleasure lies in the ball itself and in the joys of movement. Nobody ever won and nobody ever lost because the game went on forever. I might point out that I had clean-bowled John with a ball bowled from my left – wrong – hand; he might counter-propose that most of the ones I had bowled with my right hand required a fair amount of fetching. But that's as far as it went.

It was an experiment in sporting equality conducted by unequals. I seem to remember John's best shot as a windmilling hoick to leg, but let's dignify it by calling it a front-foot pull. Certainly it tended to send the ball sailing towards Streatham Common South. My father tried to show him what-for with his leg-breaks that for years had baffled me in the garden: John put them in the general direction of The Rookery. Sometimes John's father played; sometimes there were as many as half a dozen of us: a dad or two, Roger, his little brother, one or two of John's many brothers. On these occasions we could pass the ball, when it was winter and football, and we could field when it was summer and cricket. On those occasions I liked to keep wicket. There were two or three reasons for this: I liked the diving about, it was more interesting than fielding, and I was borderline competent. I think there was also a sneaking hope going on here. Perhaps I would one day have to admit that I couldn't bat and I couldn't bowl: but in such an event I would emerge as the greatest wicketkeeper that ever pulled on a gauntlet.

Not that we had gauntlets.

I remember the endless fascination of these sporting encounters. A modern child would find such a thing baffling: after all, there are no electrical sockets on Streatham Common. Surely you only did that because there wasn't anything better to do. And that's right in a way. There wasn't anything better. There couldn't be anything better. Was it computers that changed this world forever? Was it television? Was it homework? Was it paedophiliaphobia?

It was pure sport that we played, sport untroubled by ambition or competitiveness or result. It was precisely the experience we often seek when we play sport in a more loaded context: to play with Streatham Common freedom in a real match that really matters. And it's the advice we so often want to send to the participants when we're watching big-time sport: don't play the situation! Just play the damn ball! Don't play as if you were at Wembley or Lord's or Wimbledon or at the Olympic Games: play as if you were on Streatham Common, clear on goal, one run needed for victory and only – only! – John Murtagh to beat.

The best can actually do that. There is a Zennish thing in sport: that playing in the moment, that concentration on pure action. It is the sort of thing that, in the 1999 men's singles final at Wimbledon, prompted Pete Sampras to beat Andre Agassi with a second-serve ace on the final point. What was going through your mind at that point, Pete?

It's one of my favourite press conference moments. Pete said: 'There was absolutely nothing going through my mind.' And I was enlightened. If I could have played every sporting moment as I played in that eternal duel with John on Streatham Common, my sporting life would have been very different. And I would never have been able to understand the complexities of failure, so I would never have been able to write about sport.

Incompetence matters. It is a much underrated part of life. I spent about five years of my life trying to write poems. They were awful. All of them. Occasionally one turns up, dug up with glee by an old friend, and I want to die. But I have no regrets whatsoever about writing the damn things. Striving and failing are instructive things, no matter what form they take. As a boy poet I tried to find good words, good rhythms, good thoughts: to give meaning to experience by means of words. It was at first shocking and in the end dismaying to realise that I couldn't write good poems, but trying and failing to be a poet was what made me think like a writer. Every failed poem helped me to become what I am: a professional writer, even if I practise my trade at a lower level than James Joyce and Basho. Sporting failures were equally an education: every goal I conceded, every occasion when John rearranged those three stumps. After the great trauma of Sunnyhill and the cricket match against Mr Gray's class, I was never under any illusion that sport was easy.

There I was on Streatham Common playing sport and my lack of ability didn't matter. My incompetence was just part of the landscape, like the paddling pool across the road, the groups of trees, the great green sward that swept down towards Streatham High Road and the A23, and the dark, thrilling woods that stood behind The Rookery. It was sport as an expression of friendship; sport in which my inadequacies were forgiven, to the point of becoming meaningless.

Three goals. Three: a magic number, a trinity of goals. All scored by me. And then it was me diving full length in the mud again – the mud that was the smell of childhood – a sting in the hands as a hefty shot from John was stopped in its tracks, turned round the jumpers and rolling towards the trees. I expect he put away the next one though. I owe him that.

# Chapter 3

# A Leaping Wolf

It's possible to live two lives at the same time. For a while when I was at Sunnyhill School I was also a member of the 8th Streatham Wolf Cub Pack. Every Tuesday we met in the crypt of St Peter's Church and here I was a person of substance. If I was the omega male in Mrs Holland's class, I was somewhat higher up the dominance hierarchy with the Cubs. My love for the Cubs sprang from two motives: first, it wasn't Sunnyhill, so it had to be good, and second, it was all bound up with *The Jungle Book*, the text in which the love of the Wolf Cubs was based.

Kipling's tales allowed me to set my life into a different context from school: a life in which friendships with a black panther, a bear and vast python were possible, in which great battles against a tiger could be won. This was a passion unshared: few other members of the pack had actually read the sacred text, but that made it all the more vivid for me, allowing me to enter another of those kingdoms of the imagination. I was more of a wolf than any of the other Cubs. I was filled with ambition: I wanted to be the best Cub of them all. And I really was. Picture me in my last year in the pack: on my green cap, two metal stars – representing lupine eyes – which marked a certain level of achievement. Around my neck a scarf, maroon trimmed with yellow, clasped at the neck by a leather woggle that bore a wolf's mask. On the green jumper, on my left arm, five proficiency badges: Guide, House Orderly, Book-reader (perhaps not the most macho option but you have to play to your strengths), Collector, Sportsman. Over my heart, the badge of badges: the Leaping Wolf, worn only by the elite. I don't think anyone else in the pack had one. Or did David Lewis, later an officer in the navy? Surely he did. Never mind. On my right sleeve, a grey triangle demonstrated my membership of Grey Six, and, below it, two yellow bands. Yes, reader, I was Sixer of Grey Six. It is the only position of authority I have ever held in my life.

It was a damn good Six too. Most weeks we scored more points than anyone else and so it was my duty to lead the Grand Howl at the end of the evening: DYB! DYB! DYB! And no one from school had any idea that I could ever be such a person. It was only natural, then, that when the choir challenged the Cubs to a cricket match, I was the captain. I was even mad enough to believe that as a Cub, rather than a schoolboy, I would be revealed as a great batsman.

We gathered one Saturday afternoon on Streatham Common. We played on a proper cricket pitch, with white creases marked on mown grass. Half of my team were unknown to me, coming from the Wednesday night pack. Most of the choir I knew by sight, and they were mostly a year or so older. It was a little daunting. They looked a tough bunch, those trebles and altos who on Sunday sang the Agnus from the Coronation Mass with such sweetness.

Since I was captain I put myself down to bat first drop, like Ted Dexter, the captain of England. I also decided to keep wicket. It was here that my powers of leadership were tested and found wanting. One of the Wednesday Cubs told me that he, too, was a wicketkeeper, and that he had been preparing to keep wicket for the Cubs ever since the match was announced. So I proposed a weak-minded compromise: he would keep wicket for the first few overs and then I would take over. And that, it seemed to me, was where the real contest lay.

Strange what things stick in the memory. He was shorter than me, which was pretty short, thickset, chubby-faced, uncomely. He owned a pair of chamois leather inners, treasured relics, which he wore instead of the gauntlets that came in the big bag of borrowed cricket gear. And he did poorly. Not disastrously, but he was no great shakes. So I took over when my time came, strapped on the pads and put on the gauntlets. I think it was the first time I had ever worn a pair. I remember the stiff leather, the rubber caps at the fingertips, the feeling of my hands being somewhat lost, the pimpled rubber palms and fingers that looked and smelt like the ping-pong bats at home. I remember the deeply satisfying noise they made when I clapped. I remember, too, beating my palms together with my fingers pointing in opposite directions, the better to drive my fingers deep into the gloves, to get my fingertips into those rubber cups.

Perhaps I should have taken it the first time. The ball struck the bat and looped up, going at a reasonable lick, and I leapt (a leaping wolf) and found it beyond my reach. I just about managed to tip it with my deeply protected fingertips, landed off balance and falling, but sprang again as the deflected ball fell. I can still remember all this, in what, as I learned years later, sports psychologists call psychokinetic memory. That is to say I don't remember it with my mind, like reading a book or looking at a photograph, but with muscles and bones and sinews: as a thing of movement. My sporting memories – everybody's sporting memories – are full of these psychokinetic moments, moments which stand out with microscopic clarity from the great blur of the times past. I suspect such moments last to the grave. Many people reach a stage of life when it takes them a moment to recall the name of the person they had such an agreeable lunch with last week, but they can still remember in the most convoluted detail, precisely what it was like scoring a goal 60 or 70 years earlier.

I thought I had lost the damn thing but I hadn't. I remember – precisely – what it was like grabbing it again on the way down, two hands, vast gauntlets snapping on the hard red ball like the jaws of an alligator before I crash-landed on the grass. I remember that I shouted one word at the top of my voice, lest there should be any doubt: 'Held!'

He was out, then. Perhaps I had made the catch harder than it was, or perhaps it was only made possible by this complex double-shuffle, the first movement to bring it into range and the second to snaffle it. Nevertheless and whatever, it was a diving catch and I, captain and wicketkeeper, had held it.

A little later I took another catch: a dolly, but I took it with a nonchalance that surprised me only later. I also pulled off a run-out, gathering a half-decent throw with adequate tidiness and breaking the stumps. It was almost enough to console me for my latest failure as a batsman. Bad luck, the grown-ups said. Bad luck. I liked to think they had a point, and tried to build a picture of myself as a great batsman who was somehow unlucky: somehow always getting a straight ball just at the moment I was about to break free of the chrysalis of incompetence and take wing as the cricketer I was born to be.

The trouble with sport is that such notions can't survive the testing. I knew that even as a Cub, even as the Sixer of the Grey Six, even as the only Cub in the Pack (apart from David Lewis) with a Leaping Wolf, that I was never going to find competence as a batsman. And that turned out to be wrong, but it was a long old while before I reached such a point.

I loved my afternoon as the Wolf Cubs' gauntlet-banging wicketkeeper though – perhaps especially because – I knew they would never let me take the gauntlets at Sunnyhill. I loved the moment when I stood up from making that catch and saw the team around me so delighted and so surprised. Perhaps they were surprised that anyone could pull off such a catch; perhaps they were just surprised that I did. But no matter, I had done something good on the field of sport and that was miracle enough to last for an entire summer. Or a lifetime, as you see.

It is also worth pondering on the miracle of being two people at once. I'm pretty certain that if by some twisted circumstance I had been handed the gauntlets at school, I would have dropped that catch. At school they would have expected me to drop it: and I would have expected to drop it myself. At the Cubs, they expected me to catch it, and I shared that expectation. In sympathetic circumstances I was not only better: I was different.

We lost the match, of course. The choir were too good. They could sing the Agnus divinely but they refused to have mercy upon us. They bowled too fast and too straight: a lethal combination up to a pretty high level in cricket, and not to be despised at the very top. It was a mismatch, but we did all right, and three of the choristers had me to thank for their dismissal.

If only life could be like that. If only I could carry my Cubbing self out into real life; if only I could play sport against the world as I did when I was keeping wicket for the Cubs. The mysteries of teams and circumstance and motivation were all around me. Why does a great player in one team become a failure when he joins another? Do the new people want him to fail? Why does a second-rate player become a first-rate player when nothing has changed but the context in which he plays? How come some players score century after century for their counties and only ever fail when they play for England? I was beginning to realise that sport is not a simple matter; though I was also beginning to realise that if you could convince yourself that sport really was a simple matter, you'd be in a good position for doing it better.

# Chapter 4

# God on Our Side

The move to 4 The Terrace, Hill House Road, was fairly momentous. We left our little flat in Oakdale Road, went to the roomy house near Streatham Common and expanded our ideas about living. I had a room of my own where I could without disturbance read Alf Gover's *How to Play Cricket*, in the devout belief that if I read enough I could become a cricketer; in the devout belief that if I read it often enough I could change myself and the world I lived in. I wonder if I've grown out of that. Or if anybody ever does.

Downstairs there was a long sitting room with French windows, also a kitchen with adjoining breakfast room. The door between these got jammed; my father, fresh from watching *Z Cars*, charged it down in the manner of PC Bob Steele and brought a good deal of the wall down as well. If that gives the impression of a man of impetuosity, one not by nature given to the consideration of consequences, it will suffice. I wish I could remember the exact words my mother used to express her displeasure: few could concoct a disapproving phrase with her proficiency. My father was 22 when I was born; four years later he was a father of three, by which time he had acquired a proper job at the BBC, setting off on a path that led to glorious professional fulfilment.

The house was Edwardian Tudor and my parents filled it with Edwardian and late-Victorian furniture, mainly because it was all they could afford. Such stuff was regarded as dross. For the sum of seven pounds and ten shillings, my father bought a table for the dining room. Yes, we had a whole room just for eating in, an almost impossible luxury. Or not just. The table was six feet wide, in three leaves, and, when fully extended, as it always was back then, it was a good eight feet long. It was ripe for ping-pong.

My father got hold of a sort of full-sized ping-pong table top. First put a blanket down on the dining table, then the two halves of the ping-pong table. The end with the bay window was best, with the light behind you and more room to move; the other end was cramped to begin with and became even more so when we got the piano. And it was one of the world's great sporting arenas.

My father and I began to play at once. I had no idea what to do: the whole thing was new to me. It began with high bouncing rallies in which I pushed suspiciously at every ball with my backhand, and my father would pat it back, gently and kindly. In this way I acquired the beginnings of competence. But every now and then my father, unable to resist, would play a proper shot. He had two of these. One was his side-spinner, a great lateral U-shaped scoop. The ball would land on my side travelling forwards and then dive to my left as if struck by some unseen agency. To me it was the mystery of mysteries. The other was a shot I have never seen anyone else play. It was a forehand topspin played with the bat pointing down; roughly the same action with which Tony stabs Bernardo in *West Side Story*. When he caught it right, it was as if the ball had been fired from a gun. It was a revelation of undreamt of sporting possibilities.

Naturally, John Murtagh and I took up the game as well. We played all the time, when it was too dark or too wet to play on the common. How many millions of points did we play? Or billions? Here there was some equality. I had the edge in quickness and no doubt in practice time.

Ping-pong is essentially a domestic game. You play because you have a table at home, in the garage, in the basement; and each person, each household, develops idiosyncrasies of style and method. These things are only rarely taken out into the wider world. Thus everyone is champion of the world: a basement king, a monarch of the garage. You are a champion because you are unchallenged. You don't really want to do it in public: it's an essentially personal and domestic matter. A bit like sex.

Learning to play ping-pong is about learning to spin. The first breakthrough comes when you start to use your forehand, the second when you begin to use that forehand as a weapon.

Instinct. A word used all the time in sport. An instinctive save, an instinctive shot. But it's not the right word. An instinct is hardwired from birth. It's instinct that makes you flinch from danger or stretch out a hand to stop yourself falling. Most of the actions of sport fail to fit into that category. You have to learn them. When you take up a sport, you are not just trying to acquire certain skills. You are trying to embed these skills so deeply that your body responds to a situation without reference to your conscious mind. It looks like instinct, it even feels like instinct, but it's not. It's an acquired trait.

What you have done is short-circuit the usual processes, so that you act without the need to think first. All your thinking has been done before in practice and in previous matches. Thus I learned to play a chop to a top-spinner because when I tried something else I tended to miss. Thus by action you shape your responses; by doing you change who you are. Not reading, then. Action.

The written word will only get you so far; in sport and no doubt in life. Muscles have memories as well as minds. Thinking is good, but sometimes *not* thinking is better. But right actions come from right preparation.

A disputed point. John and I had disputes, but they were never bitter. So we played the point again, and John won.

'That proves it.'

'Proves what?'

'That I was right.'

'How come?'

'Because God was on my side.'

'I think God's got better things to do than umpire our ping-pong match.'

The memory is a true one. If the phrasing sounds precocious, blame my mother. And I was right: God isn't terribly interested in ping-pong, or in any sport. There's a story about Yogi Berra, the great baseball catcher, responding to an opposing batter who marked a cross with the toe-end of his bat on the home plate before preparing to face the pitcher. 'Why don't we just let Him enjoy the game?' Berra suggested.

Years later, I met Jonathan Edwards, who made such a parade of his Christian beliefs. I watched him soar to a gold medal in the triple jump at the Sydney Olympic Games in 2000, and in the piece I wrote I quoted a devotional song, one based on Psalm 91 and Isaiah: 'And He will raise you up on eagle's wings'. A great night indeed. But Edwards had a crisis of faith after he retired from athletics: and said that he realised that all the belief stuff had just been a motivational tool. Without sport he no longer needed God. When he no longer required eagle's wings he could do away with God.

I saw the fallacy of God as a judge and controller of sport before I reached my teens; perhaps it was failure that allowed me to do so. I was a religious boy, as was John; for me St Peter's Streatham was more than a meeting place for the Cubs. But I knew damn well that God wasn't about to show me any favours in the way of sporting talent and sporting victory. In sport, I was on my own. Prayer wasn't going to make me a Test cricketer, or any kind of cricketer.

But then, as another of my father's when-you're-a-Jet-you're-a-Jet top-spinners whistled past me, I thought to myself: what would it be like to play one of those? What would it be like to play a forehand that went howling past my opponent's bat as if it had a hole in it? What if I had a shot that my father couldn't possibly return? Would I feel as if God was, after all, on my side? Or would I feel just a little bit like God Himself? I thought the experiment was worth trying. So I practised.

# Chapter 5

# Top of the Tree

When is a sport not a sport? A question that failed to pursue us across Streatham Common, for as far as we were concerned it was all one and entirely seamless. Is sport only sport when it's a competition? Only sport where there is a winner and a loser? Or is it also a sport when victory and defeat are vague and elusive concepts, when victory is not necessarily sought and if found not necessarily celebrated; when defeat is not entirely avoided at all costs, and may not even be painful?

You could cross Streatham Common South by the paddling pool and beyond it lay a world of adventure. It lay within a wood. An endless expanse of forest – trees and trees and trees – and John and I were on intimate terms with them all. We climbed every one that was capable of taking a hand or a plimsoll. First move: jump to seize the lowest branch. Face the trunk, link fingers and then smear your feet up the trunk until your plimsolls are higher than your head and you can crook your right knee over the branch. From there, you make a complex squirming movement to sit astride your branch – the hardest and most important skill in tree-climbing. We used to call the whole process the Sloth. Some trees were easy, some were hard, some were devilish: no matter, we climbed them all. In some trees the branches formed a kind of staircase: it was a pleasure to climb them and climb them again because they were so inviting, because the rhythm of ascending them was so pleasing. It was as if the tree itself was obliging you personally: a tree's tribute to a climber. But some were rather more challenging: daring you to repeat the Sloth manoeuvre when you were already 20 or more feet up.

Stick close to the trunk: that was a sound enough principle. But like all sound principles it was always a pleasure to abandon it. Some of the trees were generously wide and their spreading branches were stout and accommodating; and with such trees it was stimulating to go as far towards the tip of these branches as you dared, to feel them dip and sway beneath you. When you reached their or your limit, you could lower yourself and hang from the branch, now bouncing under your weight, and time your release with a dipping downswing to land feet first and rolling in the leaf litter below. Sometimes from quite a long way up.

We had falls, of course we did. I have one clear memory: coming off a tree backwards, lashing out with a right hand – instinctively – and clutching a passing branch. It didn't stop my fall but it certainly straightened it: I remember the wrench of my shoulder and the burning of my hand, and then a landing, more or less on two feet as I rolled in a – I think again instinctive – breakfall.

Some of the trees had names. One, the Pigeon Tree, gave us the willies. It was called the Pigeon Tree because the first time we climbed it we disturbed a pigeon, which had assumed that the height and fragility of its retreat had made the place safe from panting boys. It was very hard to get into the lower branches of this tree, but once you were there it was both challenging and inviting. Each next step was hard, but within our compass. And instead of offering ever-skinnier branches, like most trees, it kept offering another interesting problem. So almost despite myself, I would find myself getting higher and higher and higher. More than once I had to make a complete circuit of the trunk as I climbed. There was one really alarming bit where I used a dead branch to complete my 360. But once I was as high as I could be, I could look out across the common and feel a sense of wild delight in my skill and daring: in the sense of being alive and at the top of the tallest tree in Streatham.

I remember the last time we made the ascent of the Pigeon Tree. We could no longer get to the top. The dead branch was no longer there. Had it fallen spontaneously, as the tree falls in the wood when there's no one there to hear it? Or had it cracked beneath the foot of another boy climber? Precipitating him to the floor so far beneath? I was frightened then, but not by my current situation. I was frightened in retrospect, by all the climbs I had made in safety long before.

Nerve is a funny thing. No one really understands it. No one likes to speak about it. If you think about it, you fear you won't be able to do it any more. Don't let the rational mind get involved: keep it as a thing of bodies and movement.

In the same mysterious way you can lose your nerve, and for no apparent reason. You can't understand the process of losing it any more than you can understand the nerve that allowed you to do it in the first place. I remember climbing a tree in my early 20s, just for the hell of it, and I was useless. Couldn't make myself do it properly. No nerve.

Left it in the Pigeon Tree all those years ago.

I was to find out a great deal more about nerve when, much later, I acquired a taste for sports more perilous than ping-pong – and then I understood that a lot of big-time sport is about the mysteries of fear and courage and their eternally complex interrelationship. It was in the trees of Streatham Common that I first got the idea that maybe all sport is a kind of courage-opp: an opportunity to find or to use parts of your personality that you don't need for everyday life. Later still, as you will see, I realised that sporting courage is not the highest or the purest form of courage. Nor is it even close. It just sometimes looks and feels that way, and that is one explanation of sport's eternal appeal to both the spectator and the doer.

Climbing rocks and mountains is usually considered a sport. It's not necessarily a competition but it's certainly an adventure with no particular point to it other than the adventure: the desire to put body and wits to the test. It's not about trying to beat the wild world; it's more an impulse to get closer to it. Riding horses, sailing boats, skiing, running: so many sports have their origin not just as a way of beating somebody but in testing yourself by doing something beautiful. Beautiful for its own sake: winning and losing being secondary considerations or no consideration at all. Beautiful, too, for the taste of courage that comes with it. I never beat John at tree-climbing, nor he me. Some trees he was better at, with his greater strength and reach; with others I was better because of my agility. It was an adventure and a better one for being shared. Perhaps all non-confrontational sports are based on something that's glorious simply to do. You can spatchcock a competition on to it as a kind of afterthought, but it begins with the simple pleasure of doing it.

There was a copper beech tree, a mighty thing, in the parkland that lay on the far side of the woods, and this had branches that seemed to stretch out to all eternity. Here it was possible to walk out along a branch while holding on to the one above. The fun was in pushing this walk as far as you dared. Once you'd reach the swaying, dipping limits of the two branches you had a choice. You could retreat, and go back the way you had come, feeling the bending branch get stronger with each step, itself a satisfying business. But you could also get down the hard way, with a bit of a flourish, without retreating at all. You turned sideways, and jumped from the lower branch while keeping hold of the higher one, swinging out and away; and at the far reach of your swing you let go, missing the reaching branches below you, landing on your toes and in the same instant making a rolling breakfall on to the fallen leaves and beech mast. And then you moved away damn quick because above there's John, and he's going to do the same manoeuvre.

# Chapter 6

# The Honours Book

Colonel Hill was head of the Lower School. He was also our geography teacher. I was now at Emanuel School, hard by Clapham Junction. Life had given me one of those priceless opportunities to throw a double six and start again, for no one from Sunnyhill had come with me. I was working hard on personal reinvention, but Colonel Hill was a problem in this project. Projects: that was the big thing for Colonel Hill: test the boys' initiative and all that. I didn't seem to have much. Those who did well in one of his projects were invited to sign the Honours Book, not a thing I ever managed myself.

Colonel Hill was a silly man in many ways, given to ingratiating self-caricature and to throwing chalk at boys who irritated him. On occasions he threw the board rubber instead – whatever was nearer to hand – a great sharp-edged block of wood capable of dealing out contusions and concussions with ease. He was a pretty good shot.

He was terribly keen on his football-map project. We were each required to put together a map of England, one that noted the location of all the 92 clubs that made up what was then the Football League. This would reveal the centres of population, by definition (back then) the centres of industry. Thus we would understand how England worked. The map would show us where the working classes were concentrated. Though the Colonel put that in other words.

Those who did well in this project got their reward of a high mark and the beaming approval of Colonel Hill, perhaps even a temporary board-rubber truce, but they were not invited to sign the Honours Book. This was because the headmaster disapproved of the project. He said that it 'encouraged an interest in Association Football'. That was clearly a bad thing.

I remember my puzzlement. I was prepared to accept anything the new school could ask of me since it offered me a new start, but I didn't understand why football was by definition a bad thing. Not that I had any special love of the game: we weren't a footballing family. My father, from Wigan, loved rugby league and cricket, Wigan and Lancashire. It seemed odd to make a moral stand about football.

I didn't understand then that this moral stand was really a social stand, and that if you can be persuaded to understand that in the right way, you realise that the two things are really one. So: rugby union teaches good morals, and association football doesn't. In other words, we weren't supposed to be boys from those footballing areas on the map.

But we were. A good few came from council housing, for a start, some of whom became great mates. The school knew that, but its aim was to drag us upwards in a social – I'm sorry, I mean moral – sense. And that, dear boys, is what education is all about, is it not?

Emanuel School was part-maintained. To explain that succinctly, it was a state school pretending it was still a public (i.e. private) school. It reverted to independence after the educational reforms of the seventies, and now offers a fee-paying education, often to sons and now daughters of expatriates stationed in London. As an educational establishment it has charitable status: in short, it's a tax-free business. Which is highly moral.

We were a rugby school. We weren't like the schools that played – ah – *other sports* in the winter. This was made very clear to us very early on. It followed then that rugby – the game itself – was something very special indeed. Almost magical. Certainly capable of making new boys of us. And so, on our first games day, we were taught the laws of rugby union: that is to say, initiated into a new form of existence: given a new set of aspirations, social and moral. Though they didn't put it like that. You could only pass the ball backwards. That was presented as a sort of moral point, as if you would only make progress by retreating. It was all very mysterious, and not without its own excitement. From now on, rugby was to define us. It showed us that we were better than the rest.

So having been taught the laws, we were sent out on to a field to abide by them. I was thrilled by this new adventure. After all, there remained the thought that this would turn out to be the game I was good at; the one game for which all my previous disappointments had been a preparation. A special school, a special game: surely it was made for me. A new world was opening up before my eyes.

Alas, my enthusiasm for rugby failed to survive the afternoon. Disillusionment was that swift. Enthusiasm didn't really survive the first tackle I attempted, when I went in hopelessly late and got a faceful of studs. It became clear within a few minutes that the bigger you are the more you enjoy rugby, in direct contradiction of what we had just been told. I was the youngest person in my class, and by a distance the smallest. The people who decided that rugby union was the ideal way to instil manly virtues in boys had clearly not come to terms with the fact that boys grow at different rates. My class contained some hulking great fellows almost ready to shave, a bunch of medium-sized boys, and two or three like me. Enthusiasm for our new sport could be equated pretty directly with physical size. Perhaps that was the idea. Perhaps it goes back to prehistory, when middle-class boys were better nourished than boys from the working-class areas of the football map, and so they were bigger and stronger. That gave them an advantage – a zing of superiority – right from the start.

I tried to be a brilliant elusive runner. I had the tricks but not the speed, nor the taste for physical conflict. I was hardly alone in my disappointment. It was an afternoon on which dreams died by the dozen. Just about everybody whose jury was out when it came to team sport had come down as an anti before they got changed back into the school uniform, a herring-bone suit with short trousers.

A more inappropriate game for a class of ten-year-olds could hardly be devised. Compulsory games are supposed to unite boys by means of a sense of shared endeavour and common purpose: this afternoon was utterly divisive. For a third of the boys who stepped out that afternoon as rugby virgins, it was a great new adventure. For another third it excited mild dislike, at best indifference. For the final third it was a sense of complete alienation: from rugby, from classmates, from school, from sport.

But it's not fair, sir. Constant cry of schoolboys throughout the centuries.

It's an unfair world, Barnes. I could forgive anything in the reply but the smugness. Of course it's unfair, but isn't it the job of those in authority to try and make it fairer? And isn't sport all about the virtues of fairness: level playing field and all that? Of course, rugby at schoolboy level is designed to show you that life is unfair and that you are the one with an unfair advantage. It was a lesson, and a highly useful one, in the way that life operates. It was also a lesson that sport is never pure and rarely simple, and that in English life, even – or perhaps especially – on the field of sport, the great English obsessions with class can always be found.

Not that I appreciated these lessons back then. I just felt that sport had been taken away from me, that I had been barred from paradise. Sport was for the sporty, not for the likes of me.

# Chapter 7

# Semi-naked
# Semi-courage

Sport is about courage. That's why we do it; we want to test our courage, and, perhaps more, we want to savour such courage as we possess. It's also why we watch the stuff. The spectacle of courage in action is compelling at a very deep level. Sport, as I first understood in the trees of Streatham Common, is a courage-opp, and one of the first things you learn when you try and do sport yourself is that courage is not a simple thing. No: it's mysterious, protean, perpetually surprising. I began to get an inkling of this truth in the gym at school.

I was a coward on the rugby field, though I was hardly alone in this. But in the gym I could appal people with my courage. Before every gym lesson began I would shin up the stout climbing bars to the top, about 20 feet from the ground, and here I would spin head over heels around the highest bar. No one else could do this: my small size was for once an asset, and so was my tree-climbing experience. True, I was regarded as a silly ass rather than a paragon of courage, and I wasn't inclined to value this feat too highly myself, since so little prestige attached to it. But it was good to irritate so many people with so little effort. Get down, Barnes, you bloody fool, people said, uncomfortable with the spectacle. But I would spin through the bars again to make them look away in vicarious vertigo.

Mr Cooper taught us gym. He was not the gym teacher of tradition: he was decent, inclusive, cheerful, encouraging. And I could do it. I was agile, physically confident, in some areas even bold. Mr Cooper formed the Gym Club and on one, maybe two, lunchtimes a week I would work on gymnastic skills. I progressed: handspring, the harder flyspring with a double-footed take-off. Soon I could link a few of these tumbles together with headspring, neckspring, forward roll. We moved on to vaulting: a headspring over a low, padded box, and then, using a springboard, we did the same thing with the box now raised to five feet. It was heady stuff, learning these skills: the strong lash of the legs you need to perform a headspring from the floor, the more studied movement from the low box, and the controlled, almost languorous unwinding you require when performing the headspring from a height. Too much leg whip and you're landing on your face. It's all about controlling your body in the air: an understanding of three-dimensional space. So then, for added difficulty – in search of added courage – you turn the high box longways, so you must dive the full length of it, four feet or so, before touching down on the top, first hands then head, flipping your legs forward as you do so – but slowly, with control, so avoiding that face-first landing – to touch down feet first, ideally fully upright with arms extended.

The Gym Club gave displays on Speech Day and other holy days of obligation, always concluding with stream-vaulting. We ran at the box in three lines, and vaulted in rapid succession, first one down the middle, then one down the right diagonal and one more on the left, three and three and three, in a great detonation of movement and agility, the box never without a vaulter for more than a second, if at all. At first I was a down-the-middler but was later promoted to the diagonals. The nature of the spectacle was significantly altered in my second year by the incoming headmaster, Mr Kuper. More or less as his first move on arrival, he banned the T-shirt from the gym. From now on all gymnastics must be performed topless: naked but for a pair of white shorts. Thus the headmaster revealed rather more of himself than he did of us.

So here in the gym was sport. Here was something I enjoyed, something I could actually do, and do better than quite a lot of other boys. I greatly enjoyed it but even early on I had to come to terms with my shortfall in ability. And also with the fact that my shortfall in ability was directly linked to my shortfall in courage. I was never able to perform a somersault: to take to the air, go heels over head and then land on my feet. I had the right build and just about enough strength to get all the height I needed from a springboard, but I lacked whatever it was that I needed to commit to the manoeuvre. Perhaps with a bit more coaching I could have managed it, but Mr Cooper had half a dozen or more boys who could somersault for fun. I remember the awe in which I held Jim Hewson and Rod Ball who were bold enough to get real height from the take-off and unwind the somersault almost in slow motion. Both learned to do a front somersault piked: that is to say with straight legs, arms extended to make a fine body shape. They looked as if they were flying: and I knew that their skill, their courage were beyond mine. It is always useful to learn about courage and particularly about where yours ends. In the gym I was brave *ma non troppo*.

I was able to master the short-arm overswing on the long box, an alarming trick that requires you to overshoot and perform the manoeuvre with your head below the level of the box's padded top. But I lacked the strength in the arms to perform the much more graceful long-arm overswing. And then there was Newman.

I can't remember his first name: we were supposed to address each other by surnames. He had no great prestige in the school, but he could perform the falling leaf and that was one of the most remarkable feats of sporting courage I have ever seen. No one else could do it and, what's more, no one else even tried. He would sit on a beam close to the roof, more or less as high as I would climb for my round-the-bars trick. Newman would make himself comfortable on his beam, legs extended. And then he would fall. Backwards. Just let himself go and as he did so, he would gracefully flip his feet over his head and land on his toes 15 feet below. Mr Cooper would always stand beneath him ready to catch him should Newman get it wrong, but he never did. Courage, commitment, the sort of control that comes from the ability to make your own safety a comparatively low priority: this was wonderful, but beyond my scope and, indeed, my ambition.

But I had – I'm rather ashamed to admit – a showstopper trick of my own. It was a combination of such skill and nerve as I possessed in the gym, and the deeply regrettable taste I had for clowning in my first year or two at Emanuel. First I would run at the box, which was presented longways. I would bounce on the springboard and land in a headstand at the nearer end of the box: not easy, you need to decelerate from spring to standstill in an instant of time. From there I would walk on my head to the far end of the box and then headspring to the floor, landing on my feet. I would perform the headwalk by lifting my head from the top of the box and nudging forward a few inches, and then letting go with my hands to follow my head, and so, in this series of double shuffles, I would reach the far end of the box, where Mr Lewis – by then in charge of gymnastics – would warn me to stop shuffling and spring down. It was the individual star turn of the gym display, and once it was done we would swing the box sideways and conclude with the traditional stream-vaulting, the headmaster beaming at our semi-nudity, our athleticism, our skill, our courage. Such as it was.

# Chapter 8

# For the Love of Violence

We played ping-pong at school, but never in an organised fashion. Tables were sometimes set up in the gym, and we played informally, mostly in the lunch hour, bringing our skills from garage, basement and dining room out into the open. Most of us learned that we were not as good as we had hoped, but that's kind of the idea of sport. At least partly. You test yourself at one level, and if you are good enough you try at a higher level and fail. Or not, of course.

It was in these circumstances that I learned to play the forehand loop. This is the shot at the heart of ping-pong; at the heart of table tennis at whatever level the game is played. It's a radical change from everything you try to do at the beginning, when the challenge is to keep the ball on the table. At the start you play the game in a series of gentle backhand pokes. Once you begin to play the forehand loop you find yourself hitting the ball as hard as you can. You hit the ball as if you were trying to knock it clean through the dining-room wall. But you don't play *through* the ball, like a batsman playing a cover drive: you play *across* it, imparting millions of revs on the ball. That's what brings it down on to the table, instead of flying off into space. It travels in an arc, rather than a loop, and there's nothing easy or gradual about it.

In tactical terms, it's a simple equation at this level of the game: if I landed the ball on the table with a forehand loop, I won the point. The snag was that it didn't come off every single time. I realised, then, that I had to be smart: only play the loop when there was a very good chance of pulling it off. A nice high ball to the right of your body: just the job. Alas, I wasn't smart. As my father burst through the kitchen door, so I would smash when blocking was more advisable. Sometimes, it's true, I would get a fast low ball and slam it back at the speed of sound, watching it pause for an instant to kiss the far side of the table before vanishing into the far reaches of the gym. But more often I would snag the ball in the net or send it soaring like a little planet up towards the high spaces where I used to spin around the highest bar. I could put away an inviting, floaty ball with fair reliability – say, seven times in ten – but sometimes, when my opponent played a shot that was begging for the cruellest dispatch, I would become hopelessly overeager and miss. So I found myself vulnerable to both good shots and bad shots: to easy balls and to difficult balls.

But I carried on playing the same way. I never tried to amend my game. As a result of this, it gradually became clear to me that winning was not the deepest pleasure the game had to offer. At least to me. I loved my forehand loop far too much. The pleasure of playing it to a routine smashable ball was deep enough; playing it to a really good shot was an even greater thing, a really profound kind of joy. A smash to the corner, and you smash it back to the table at full stretch. No victory could touch that for pleasure.

So it became clear that there was something amiss in my approach to sport. Sport is not just about being good at playing, it's also about being good at winning. It's a quite separate talent. You can be the best actor in the world and fail to get a job because you aren't good at auditions and the business of selling yourself. In short, you lack the talent for having talent. I understood then that you need more than sporting excellence to win at sport. You also need the talent for victory. I have seen these two things come together at the greatest moments that sport can provide: and I know that was what I was watching because I knew too well the failure in myself.

Of course, I won a fair few matches here and there. I wasn't bad, but I was always prone to getting sidetracked, and it was the loop that sidetracked me. Thus my greatest strength was my greatest weakness, and I have seen that basic truth of sport in top-level competition a million times over.

I thought about this. That's when I learned that thinking can be a terrible mistake in sport. When you start thinking you lose the ability to short-circuit conscious thought. I pondered the eternal question of looping and not looping – sticking and twisting – going for it and holding back – and as I did so I began to develop an inability to win. I can understand this in retrospect as Reverse Sampras Syndrome: there was always far too much going through my head, never the desired nothing.

So I would lead 18–12 with my forehand almost literally a lethal weapon, and then I would lose 21–19. I would alternate excessive caution with excessive aggression: first poking back a ball that begged to be slammed and then slamming a ball that required a good deep safe return. You can see the same approach in cricketers overwhelmed by the situation: block, block, slog, the quality and the nature of the ball delivered playing no part at all in the decision-making process.

My inability to win reached a peak on family holidays to Cornwall. There was a building with a ping-pong table and plenty of room, and here the children, offspring of a dozen holidaying families, would gather. Given half a chance I would lose by a couple of points against all comers. I would take on a really good player, play out of my skin and lose by the odd point: I would take on a no-hoper and be overcome by incompetence. Thus I began to understand various unexpected things about the nature of sporting ability.

I began to see that champions in these one-on-one sports require a high and lonely sort of courage. They must first believe that what they want matters a great deal more than anybody else's convenience and anybody else's feelings. They must be perpetually indifferent to the distress they cause their opponents. People called Roger Federer an artist: don't tell that to the people he routinely beat at his best. To them he was a torturer. Of course, Federer is the supreme example of a tennis player who loves the game for its own sake, rather than as a vehicle for victory and self-aggrandisement, and that is why he is universally admired and loved. But he couldn't have used that method with such success had he not been absolutely relaxed about the business of causing dismay in other people. Federer has never shirked the task of causing his opponent pain.

People will say of a player in any sport: 'He's too nice.' This is a heresy: against both sport and against niceness. I wasn't too nice. I was too deferential. Too weak. Too ingratiating. Niceness and deference aren't the same thing at all; nor are niceness and weakness.

It's all in the way these things take you. Those who know me in professional life will laugh at the idea of me as a deferential, easy-going person. I remember reporting to a sports editor at the start of the Olympic Games: 'We're a very nice team, all good writers, all decent people, and no big egos apart from me.' Which just about summed it up. But my colleagues could probably all have beaten me at ping-pong. In other words sport reveals character – but not all of it.

I was a better at doubles than singles, because that way I craved the approval of my partner more than that of my opponent. That puts it crudely, but there's an essential truth in that. Standing alone – at least in sporting terms – was not something I was ever going to be good at. Is that innate? Just as the kind of coordination you need to play sport well is innate? Certainly both can be developed: there is coaching, there is sporting psychology, there is also the rough-and-ready system in which we seek to improve ourselves without reference to specialists.

So which comes first? And which matters more? Is it the ability to play good shots, or the ability to win without compunction?

Big questions. But to hell with them: I could play a forehand loop and that was joy enough. I played it against John Murtagh, which was great, except that John was developing skills of his own. The standard of our ping-pong soared, especially when I had the window end. These battles – or perhaps it was one unending battle – were a profound joy. The pleasure of ping-pong was not that it allowed me to beat someone, but that it allowed me to play the forehand loop: right wrist, elbow, shoulder, the whole body committed to the shot, an act of violence unfeasible in normal life: violence meted out to an absurd piece of celluloid that couldn't hurt anybody if it was fired from a gun. That is the intoxicating secret of ping-pong, that profound contradiction in which you use massive violence for an almost negligible result. But there it is: the ball bouncing high in the right-hand corner and sitting above the table surface – better still, a little behind it – and there am I bringing the bat up from the height of my knees and swinging it in a great bravura arc of 180 degrees, the follow-through way above my head. And the ball is speeding to its destiny, sometimes catching the far corner of the table as it does so, at other times snagging in the net like a salmon that missed its leap, or crashing into the far wall and getting lost behind the piano. One forehand loop puts all the world to rights.

In other words, I hadn't got the idea of sport at all. Coaches are always going on about trying to let young players play for the simple love of it during their formative years, and that's great if you don't want to remove all the originality from a person, from a player. But ultimately when it comes to competition you have be able to beat people, and to do so without inhibition. Anyone who has ever had dealings with me in professional life and found me intransigent and with too good an opinion of myself can easily redress the balance: just challenge me to a game of ping-pong. I'll lose, of course I'll lose: but I'll still go away at least half satisfied. Because one or two of those forehand loops will have found their mark.

# Chapter 9

# Hell is Other Rugby Players

There's a scene in Hunter S. Thompson's *Hell's Angels* when Sheriff Baxter confronts Sonny Barger, president of the Oakland Chapter of the Hell's Angels and de facto leader of the 300 or so outlaw motorcyclists camped around Bass Lake. The sheriff says: 'There's no reason why you can't enjoy yourself here like everybody else. You guys know what you're doing. There's nothing wrong with you. We know that.'

Thompson continues the tale: 'Then Barger smiles, very faintly, but he smiles so seldom that even a grimace means he thinks something is very funny. "Come off it, Sheriff. You know we're all fuck-ups or we wouldn't be here.'"

That was precisely the way we all felt: the 100-strong crowd of us on our way to Blagdons on Thursday afternoon to play rugby: dismal, desolate and hopeless. Surely – *surely* – life wasn't supposed to be like this.

Greg Hunt was in my form or class for most of our schooldays, never an intimate, though he played my daughter – this was a boys-only school back then, remember, so sexual versatility was required in our dramatic efforts – in the Ionesco play *Jacques*. He was good at sport, and played scrum-half for the school. That meant he never had to face the horrors of Blagdons. He was too good. Alas, he died last year. Dave Debidin, who played Jacques's future mother-in-law – he was also a silky batsman for the school and subsequently for the Old Boys – suggested that a few of us meet to raise a glass to Greg's memory. Dave has gamely taken on the task of keeping us all in touch, and these days meet-ups tend to be agreeable and easy-going. So this was a good plan. Where to meet, then? Dave suggested Blagdons, where Old Emanuel traditionally played their cricket matches.

At once an emailed cry of horror went out along the string of a couple of dozen. No! Anywhere but Blagdons! No one could bear Blagdons. No one but Dave had good memories of the place. So we met at the pub at the end of the school drive and had a very pleasant evening. Which we really couldn't have managed at Blagdons, because for us Blagdons means despair.

Blagdons is Emanuel's second sports ground; it lies in New Malden, south London. On Thursday afternoons we would walk to Clapham Junction station, get the train to Raynes Park, walk a mile or so and then get changed into our rugby kit to play matches, house against house. The people who were any good at rugby stayed and played on the school ground and were groomed for stardom or played matches against other schools. So we were the rump, the arseholes, the fuck-ups. There was no disguising the fact. We knew we were all fuck-ups or we wouldn't be there.

Hardly anyone wanted to play rugby: that was the key to it. For most of us the principal goal was not victory but getting it over as quickly as possible. The secondary goal was to avoid getting muddy and thereby give the showers a miss. So try and imagine it. Rugby union is about physical commitment before anything else at all, including ball skills. Our matches were contested by two teams of 15 boys, most wishing they were doing something quite different. You can't play rugby without a relish for bodily contact: and yet we evolved a version in which contact was reduced to a minimum. Tackling would have been a serious faux pas: no one got down low despite the teacher-referee's unending instruction: 'Legs! Legs! Legs!' You must be joking, sir. If you want a boot in the face, you dive. Not me. Instead there was a little upper-body grappling, nothing very testing, but, all the same, better avoided. If you were seized at all, it was by the neck.

Rugby hinges on the idea that the ball is a precious thing, to be retained at all costs, worth any sacrifice and carefully transmitted from one pair of loving hands to another. In our games the ball was like the Black Spot: a curse, a plague, a thing to be got rid of as soon as possible. That's because if you accepted the ball you made yourself available for tackling. So let me offer you another of those traumatic childhood scenes. This one was less like Joyce or Proust, more like *Oliver Twist*. It took place on one more weary afternoon of wasted time at Blagdons, vast leaden skies, a pitch that held a tang of frost and still countless aeons would have to pass before my train at last arrived at Streatham Common; to make things still worse, an afternoon at Blagdons meant we got home an hour later than usual but with the same amount of homework.

Drake House – my lot – house colour dogshit-brown, very sexy – had the ball, a rare enough thing, and the ball was passed out along the line as rapidly as usual, and for the usual reasons. How I hated that bloody ball: enormous, awkwardly shaped, heavy, and poorly formed for kicking or passing or even just carrying. Eventually it came out to me as I ran uncertainly along the touchline. Perhaps I was playing on the wing. If so that was certainly not a tribute to my natural speed and elusiveness. You might assume that I was placed there because I was already a peripheral figure, but that would miss the point. We were all peripheral figures.

Anyway, there I was running with the ball and there ahead of me was a fellow considerably larger than me – and that doesn't narrow the field much – who clearly thought that in the case of so insignificant an opponent he might make an exception to the rule of avoiding physical contact. Perhaps I was wrong, but it wasn't a risk I was prepared to take. So I passed. Not to a team-mate, there being none within reach. I passed into touch.

I can't remember the name of the master or teacher in charge, except that he was a large fellow with a big jawline who fancied himself as a hard case. So let's call him Mr Hardcastle: he'd like that. He didn't take me for any lessons, so I didn't know him well. I was aware that people who fancy themselves as hard cases can be dangerous, even if not in the way they intend, but I also had more than a little contempt for him. And he was not impressed by my pass into touch.

'What did you do that for, Barnes?'

'I didn't want to get tackled, sir.'

This was a plain statement of fact, but it was also a rejection of everything we were supposed to be doing. It wasn't defiant: it was subversive. It was not about sport any more than Oliver Twist's request was about food. Mr Hardcastle naturally saw it as a personal attack, as such people always do, but it really wasn't. I didn't give a stuff about him. I was defying the whole bloody charade of uselessness that had us going through the motions of this stupid game at this godforsaken place when I'd sooner be back home in Streatham eating peanut butter sandwiches.

Mr Hardcastle expressed the deepest disgust at my moral character. He attempted to hold me up to shame before my team-mates and my opponents. I met all this with complete indifference, and countered with a silly-ass performance that took the heat out of things. His disgust was immense, but it had no effect on me whatsoever. His esteem was nothing to me. Nor did I lose esteem among my team-mates and opponents; if anything I was admired for my effrontery. And so I learned that you can't have sport unless people actually want to play. Like horses and water. I was prepared to make this point, out loud and in public: this is shit, and your power over me is strictly limited. You can make me go to Blagdons, you can make me put on my dogshit-brown Drake House sweater, but you can't make me enjoy it and you can't make me commit to it. I won't put my heart into this because my heart is my own and beyond your reach.

This was sport as a form of punishment, but what were we being punished for? For the crime of not being very good at sport? Double maths made for a joyless afternoon but at least there was a reason for it: an attempt to force even the least gifted of us to understand the rudiments of a subject that seemed to have some kind of importance or meaning.

But from Blagdons, what did we learn? Resentment and skiving. Resentment of sport, resentment of those who were good enough to be spared the weekly trip to New Malden. I understood then that compulsory games is an oxymoron. Like good sex, good sport can only be consensual: performed by people who are committed as a matter of choice, not compulsion. There have been experiments with compulsory sporting excellence in China and under the Soviet system, and this is a system that has broken hearts and spirits and bodies. But not those of the champions. You can come up with plenty of arguments against the Chinese production line of elite divers but you won't do so by talking to any of their serial gold medal-winners. I watched the great Fu Mingxia on many occasions, and she was one of the finest athletes I have ever met. I asked her, through an interpreter, what of the many hard and painful dry-land exercises she hated most. She gave me a Paddington Bear hard stare: 'The only exercise I don't like is one I can't do.' She may have been pressed into action, but she won on no terms other than her own.

Sport, as I knew from my adventures on Streatham Common, and I was to experience again much later, is about joy: a gleeful entering into the contest, to win, to lose or to draw but always with a full heart. And you can't have compulsory joy. Compulsory sport is like a bicycle without a rider: it can't go anywhere. It just falls over. A bicycle is only stable when in motion: sport is only possible with commitment and joy. Sport is powered by an eagerness to win, and that requires a readiness to lose. Admittedly very few top performers ever put it that way: but what do they know? Most of them have too much talent to understand sport properly; to understand sport as the world sees it, as the world plays it.

At Blagdons sport was a pre-vision of hell: an eternity of futility. It wasn't actively painful but its utter pointlessness was a deeper and more subtle torture. Some of my Blagdons colleagues – there was no opposition, we were all on the same side, all eager only to get home – took against sport for the rest of their lives, some merely against rugby union.

Sport is meritocratic; that's kind of the point. It goes back to the atavistic need to establish a dominance hierarchy. That's why sport offends people with egalitarian principles: they would prefer to come up with some kind of physical activity in which none can establish superiority over any other. Proper sport requires failure: as Gore Vidal said: 'It is not enough to succeed. Others must fail.'

Which is fair enough in its way. We, the Blagdons 100, accepted that the school's sporting elite were entitled to their sport, and we bore no resentment for our failure to be a part of it. What we hated was this crushing of spirits in this dismal waste of time.

I turned against Blagdons, for who did not? But I never turned against sport. I put that in quite another category. A part of me was still caught up with the romanticism of sport and its place in the kingdom of the imagination – and still is for that matter. I didn't see Blagdons as sport, and therefore bad. I saw it as a travesty of sport; worse, a kind of blasphemy. So I resolved to find some other path that would lead me towards my wild fanciful foolish and impractical dreams of sporting glory.

Oddly enough, it wasn't long before one such path opened out before me and I even ran along it for a little while. But then I reversed my steps, went back to the crossroads and took another path entirely.

# Chapter 10

# Death of an Athlete

I could run forever. When I wanted to go somewhere I ran. Didn't everybody? It was something of a surprise when I discovered that everybody didn't. When the school playing field was too wet to be played on, members of the junior school were instructed to run around it rather than across it. Six times round the field, we were told, then you can change and go home. It was more an initiative test for cheats than an endurance test for runners: no one kept count of the laps. It was like the caucus race in *Alice in Wonderland*: you ran a bit and you stopped when you liked. For the majority the technique of choice was to run the half in front of the school, where the teachers in charge kept an eye, and walk the other half, at the end to come jogging in, blowing conscientiously and finishing a judicious interval after the keen runners had done their stuff. Not me. I ran all six laps and ran them fast. I was always among the first few to finish. It gave me quiet pleasure, burning off all the top rugby players. None of them could live with me. I was aware, of course, that this made running a pretty poor thing, no real test of sporting ability. No prestige attached to my speed and endurance but, all the same, I looked forward to the rain, and the chance to run the legs off just about everyone in my year.

In my third year there was a slight shift in sporting emphasis. The early part of the spring term was now devoted to cross-country running. This is not an obvious term to use around Clapham Junction: the countryside we crossed was Wandsworth Common and we stuck to the pavement and the asphalt paths. Those who excelled in the tour de Wandsworth were promoted, and I was of course among them. Everybody set out at the same time, but the elite – wearing sashes around our waists so that no sluggard would make the mistake of following us – ran a longer course. I seem to remember that the leading rugby players were let off cross-country to work on their rugby skills, so it was clear what really mattered in the sporting scheme of things. I was fine with all this: faster than most, but never among the fastest.

Then came one afternoon when there was a cross-country fixture against another school or schools, and the top six from last week's run were sent out as a team. I had finished seventh, so I stayed back at school, but that was no disappointment. Instead, I saw an opportunity. I knew that nobody left in the school that day was as fast as me round Wandsworth Common. No long course this week: just a plain simple run, one size fits all, around the shorter distance.

I was aware, as never before, of my potential. I knew that I needed no pacemaker, that I need show deference to nobody. I was ready to give the entire school a lesson in running. I was wholly without anxiety at the start: little short of euphoric. Mr Hardcastle sent us off, and I was in the lead by the end of the school drive – admittedly a reasonable stretch, a couple of hundred yards.

I ran as I have never run before or, for that matter, since. I ran with freedom, certainty and joy. There was exaltation in every stride: this was what it was like, then, to be a runner. I looked over my shoulder, not in anxiety but to savour the wonder of it. Those following figures, how distant! How foolish! How futile! And I ran and ran. It seemed that my feet had been let off contact with the ground, that I was running a millimetre or so above the level of the paving stones and the asphalt. I felt as if I could run through walls, not by knocking them down but by passing between the bricks, bedazzling the mortar with sheer speed. I felt the loss of self that comes in total identification with speed, something I was not to experience again for many years, and once found again it became an addiction. Here was a strange prefiguration, in oddly twisted form, of the most important part of my sporting life. But naturally, at the time, the present was all my concern.

Many years later I was to interview Ayrton Senna, the great Brazilian racing driver, an encounter both profound and spooky, one that haunts me to this day. Senna talked about the sensation of leading a race by miles – and being impelled to look for even more, to strive for something beyond victory, perfection, to set new limits for himself and then surpass them. I felt something of the same thing, admittedly without the shadow of death: I looked for more and found I could go still faster, something I had never tried to do when running with the rest. With other proper runners in the field I would never have had the temerity to pass them, or at least I don't think so. I would never have tried to emigrate to this far and lonely country of golden movement and ever faster pace.

Leaving the Common now, into Chivalry Road, lined with cars, narrow pavement. Could there be a final effort?

Could there really be more than more? Glory, glory, glory: there really was. I was sprinting now, the wind from my own pace in my face, turn left into Battersea Rise, over the railway line, the one that would soon take me home to Streatham with a profoundly altered attitude to sport, and left into the school drive, the last 200 yards, and just as well I was running above the surface of the drive or I'd have left scorch marks on the tarmac: finally, impossibly, wonderfully, to finish in front of the main entrance to the school: alone, gloriously alone.

Alone?

Where the bloody hell was Hardcastle?

I bolted along the corridor, up the stairs to the staff room and knocked on the door, a process all teachers loathe. Hardcastle himself opened the door.

'Sir! What was my time, sir?'

A pause. A look at his watch. A thought. A conclusion. 'You cheated. You took a short cut.'

And that was the end of my running career.

I still find that a little odd. If my professional career has a theme, it's in the ancient joy of sticking it up the people who have written me off. The many people who told me I was useless, not as a motivating device but from genuine conviction, tended to bring out defiance rather than resignation. But when Hardcastle dismissed me with such contempt, I merely thought, well, fuck you.

And got on with the rest of my life.

It was in one sense typical schoolmaster. On being presented with any unusual situation, assume that the boy concerned is malicious, that he is working a scam against life in general and you in particular. That's the problem of being a hard case: you have to work on the basis that nothing is more important than your own dignity. You do this because at bottom you are afraid. I could perceive something of that even then, even in the bitterness of this rejection.

In another sense, it's typical of all people who run sport, from a schoolmaster with 100 13-year-olds in his care or the presidents of the FIFA and the IOC: sport and athletes are important only for what they can do for you. What matters at base is your own position; your own power.

It was also a lesson about lazy cynicism. It's a journalist's default position as much as it is a school-teacher's, as the above paragraph indicates. It is, it has to be said, reasonably effective: if you always think the worst of people you will never be disappointed and very seldom surprised. If you take on the role of the self-defensive cynic you will always give an impression of rough worldly wisdom.

But you will miss the good bits. When I watched Usain Bolt shatter the world record in the 100 metres at the Beijing Olympic Games in 2008, I didn't think: 'What's he on?' Rather, I felt struck by a lightning bolt of joy. I'm inclined to believe that my life is richer for this. I could see that Hardcastle's unthinking cynicism was simply the wrong approach. The way he looked at his charges and his profession was irredeemably flawed. The fact that he might have discovered a fairly decent runner didn't even occur to him.

Did I take a short cut by mistake though? I've occasionally worried about that. I was reasonably familiar with the course, but place and direction have never been very certain things for me. I have managed more than once to get lost in Manhattan, so obviously Wandsworth Common will always have its challenges. It's perfectly possible that I inadvertently cut a corner. That doesn't mean I didn't still run bloody fast, or that Hardcastle's inability to read the sincerity on my face wasn't a pretty woeful thing.

I'd like to say that it was a death of a great athlete, that Hardcastle's crassness robbed Britain of the Olympic gold medal in the marathon in Los Angeles in 1984. But I really can't go that far. If I'd really wanted to run, I could have run. I could have taken the setback in my stride, used it as motivation, emerged from the mess as an athlete of commitment and purpose and refound those glorious moments along Chivalry Road when, already running my very fastest, I upped my pace and went faster still. So all the responsibility for my athletic career is mine.

I didn't really like running that much. I didn't love it for its own sake, despite Chivalry Road. It was just a way of getting to places. I did a paper round – 13/6 a week, seven days a week – and did it all on the run. Later when the time came I spent half my life running between Streatham and Tulse Hill, because that was where lovely Christine Hill lived. But running was never a cause in itself.

It was 20 years before the jogging boom and the fashion for street races and city marathons, so running wasn't regarded as a big thing. And I knew that, no matter how fast I ran in the spring term, by the following autumn I'd still have to go to Blagdons and play rugby. I could have been Abebe Bikila – who won the Olympic marathon in 1960 and again in 1964, who ran away from the field at 30 kilometres and finished as full of running as I was that day in the school drive – and I'd still be required to play rugby.

And I was damned if I was going to do that ever again.

# Chapter 11

# One of the Elite

It was the answer to everything. I would find prestige, respect, self-respect, meaning, fulfilment. I would find swagger, identity, certainty. I would become a person of consequence. I was going to achieve all these things because I was now a member of the Boat Club. One of the elite.

Emanuel own a boathouse hard by the auspiciously named Barnes Bridge: how could I fail in such circumstances? The school was always winning prizes in regattas. Excellence in rowing was more or less a founding principal of the school. Rowing was stressed almost every time the school was placed before the public. There was serious money here, even I could see that: a boathouse full of finely made racing craft – along with a boatman to look after them – was not available to those boys from Sunnyhill who went to Dunraven or Tulse Hill or even Battersea Grammar. Our success in rowing meant that we were a cut above your normal south London school. We mattered. So I decided that I would become one of the people who did the mattering. As opposed to the rugby players, who, it was clear, didn't matter in the way that the rowers did. Rugby showed we were as good as all the other rugby schools; rowing showed we were better. So I joined the Boat Club and was ready to take my place, when the time came, among the highest of them all. It was my great bid for conformity: to take on the values of the school and what they meant in terms of social class.

I was a cox. The logic was faultless. My size was now a positive advantage. All I had to do was acquire the skills, and I was sure I had them all within me, bursting for expression. So I set up a personal campaign for acceptance by the Boat Club and I went about it scientifically. I started to go to the boathouse on Saturday morning as a volunteer. Usually there were enough of us to make an impromptu crew and we would set out in The Tub Four, a huge, unwieldy and probably unsinkable craft. Colonel Hill would give the orders from the cox's seat and I would perch behind him on the stern decking, unbelievably steering the damn thing about the Tideway.

I learned how to give the orders. Backstops! Come forward! Paddling *firm*, are you ready? Go! And off we would go, snaking erratically about the river, the crew of four pulling boyfully on their unfamiliar oars, splashing, digging, catching crabs and shooting their slides: off on the road to becoming the elite athletes of Emanuel School. Some of my crew members on these early journeys went on to contest the final of the Princess Elizabeth Cup at Henley a few years later, the biggest prize in schoolboy rowing.

Soon enough we had become the Junior A eight, and I was in charge of the damn thing with a series of coaches yelling at us from the towpath: a megaphone and a pushbike, in line with the most ancient of traditions. We were out on the river on Wednesday afternoons and Saturday mornings and there was nowhere else I wanted to be.

I loved it. I belonged. We were united: a crew: and we were committed, at least to a degree. This was better than Blagdons. We were all quite serious about trying to make the boat go faster. I expanded into the role: all right now, ten *really* firm strokes! Uh-one-aaaah! Uh-twoooo -aaaah! And on towards Kew, the river narrowing, the banks greener, the river stinking, as it did in those days, the crew slowly acquiring the balance to express the growing power of their bodies.

We did warm-up exercises, which I supervised and led, and if I could do them as well or better than the rest of the crew it was a gratifying reproach to the rest. Often we ran upstream to Chiswick Bridge, crossed and came back on the other side, returning over Barnes Bridge, the crew struggling to keep pace with their coxswain.

Then out on the water again and the ever-shifting, never-changing exhortations from the coach on the bank: sit up straight, Five, you're wobbling like a jelly in a heatwave. Two, you're still bum-shoving. Use your legs if you want to drive the boat. Cox, paddle firm as far as Chiswick Steps and wait for me there.

And I would give the orders, and we would wait for the bicycle to arrive and for the coach to assess our performance. All that talking; so many words for so simple a skill. Years later – it was early 2004 – I spent a morning cycling up and down the path alongside an artificial lake in Berkshire following a coxless four. The crew moved their boat even better than my crew moved The Tub Four. Stroke was a fellow named Matthew Pinsent, coach Jürgen Gröbler. Afterwards, when we were all gathered around on the hard, the boat back in the boathouse and the bikes in the rack, Jürgen asked me to lead the debrief. Gröbler was a brilliant coach always looking for something new, and a man not without a quiet Germanic sense of humour, as the invitation indicates. So I spoke.

'I was telling Jürgen that I was reminded of the time I rode a Grand Prix dressage horse. You're staggered by the power: that's the first thing. But then you realise that power is secondary: that it's really all about balance. If you get out of balance with a horse like that, you find you're half passing across the arena towards places you had no intention of visiting. So it's about power held in perfect balance. Without balance the power is useless. And that's what you lot looked like in that last piece of fast work: power balanced on the edge of a knife.'

They liked that, those boys. And a few months later they won the Olympic gold medal by eight 100ths of a second. They were still losing half a second from the end: but an overwhelming discharge of power – *balanced* power – changed everything in the last two or three extraordinary strokes. Bow passed bow in the final foot of the race. Naturally I claim to this day that it was my contribution to their coaching that made all the difference.

I liked it there, being in the thick of it all, these enormous men setting off on their enormous quest. I've always liked being around during training. There's a meaning in the preparation that can get obscured in the actual event. I always loved the gallops more than the racecourse.

I also liked being at Emanuel Boathouse, sharing the waters with the great men – for men they seemed – of the first eight and the second eight: the cheerful if condescending banter, the sense of being part of a shared endeavour. Once or twice a term the entire Boat Club would set off in a fleet to burn up the river at racing pace, the coaches in the school launch, the *Colonel Charles*, named for Colonel Hill, of course, seven or eight boats, each with nine boys, racing in on the flooding tide and beating the water into Guinness with the blades, the air filled with the nutmeg-grater voices of the coxes: ten *really* firm strokes now! And the first eight beat the second eight and the Colts A beat the Colts B, and, glory be, Junior A beat Junior B – take it away now, Junior A! We've got 'em now. Let's finish them with ten *really* firm strokes now ...

I had cracked it. I was at one with the sporting life at last.

## Chapter 12

# Head of the River

The river was closed to all but us schoolboys, and it was alive with our spindly craft. From a balloon floating above Hammersmith Bridge it would have looked like the mating frenzy of several hundred gigantic aquatic insects. Somewhere in the middle was Emanuel Colts A and its cox – Junior A that was, now a year older – holding station according to the number on our bow, fidgeting our way upstream, against the tide, ready to take our turn, to make a U-turn into the middle of the river and race our guts out. I was going to steer my guts out, and I was also going to shout my guts out.

This was the Schools Head of the River race: 200, maybe 300 crews, released one at a time, a few seconds between each, to race against the clock and each other. Fastest time wins it. It was and still is a great event: the Emanuel first eight was expected to be at the sharp end of the race; by 2014 they had won the race 11 times, more than any other school. This, then, was pretty serious stuff, and I was deeply worried about making a balls of the nit-picking preliminaries: to miss our slot, between crew 116 and crew 114, to get in a tangle with the little shuffling manoeuvres – one stroke bow! Hold her off, stroke! – required to keep us from running aground or drifting away from the bank.

It was the most important thing I had ever done in sport, so naturally I was pretty worked up about it. I had even spoken about this at home, and, to my surprise, my father was mildly interested. He was so concentrated on his work – he was producer of the children's television programme *Blue Peter* – that nothing outside was entirely real to him. But he listened to what I said about the race and then amazed me. 'I'm working in Hammersmith tomorrow so I'll come and watch. I'll be on Hammersmith Bridge when you go under it.' You don't go under a bridge, you shoot it, but never mind that. My father would be on the bridge as mighty Colts A did their stuff on the waters of the Tideway beneath: starting near Chiswick Eyot we would shoot Hammersmith Bridge and race to Putney, fighting off other crews all around. And we'd be great. This was, after all, our bit of river.

We came to the turning point, made our 180 – easy, stroke side. Back it down, bow side – and paddled on with the stream towards the start. The marshals' voices booming out at us. 'Right on course, 115!' I'd done all right. I'd thought I was too far across towards Middlesex, but presumably these people knew what they were about. And then we were at the start: 'Get back towards Surrey 115!' A stab of fear at this irascible voice, not my fault, the other man said to hold the course I was on. And then with a splash and crash and what passed as a roar from me we were off and racing, heading round the right-handed curve towards the bridge, with me calling the time at voice-cracking volume. Calling 'in … out' wasn't the done thing: the possible sexual interpretations were too much for adolescent boys. So the call was bowdlerised: coxes replaced 'in' with 'there'. So off we went, the crew splashing gamely and me shouting as if I wanted to set my lungs on fire: 'They-urrr … out! They-urr … out!'

The bridge was coming towards us and where was my father? As if they belonged to another being my eyes left the river and the great armada of eights and soared to the bridge, to the line of spectators watching this great parade of action and hope. I implored my crew to keep together, to push hard, to dole out ten *really* firm strokes now, and again and again my truant eyes fled to the bridge: surely I could spot my father, he'd be looking down, the graceful chains of the bridge behind him, leaning on the balustrade, eager to pick out the crew coxed by his son. Where was he? How could this be?

It was then I realised that I was well off course. I should have been under the second lamppost as we shot Hammersmith: I was nearer the fourth. Between us and the Surrey shore, as we took the long way round, rival boats were coming through, going past us on the inside in the gap I had so obligingly left them. There was no escaping it: the cox had coxed it up.

We made our way to the finish, shattered and, as I already knew, humiliated. I had probably lost us 12 lengths. We turned at the designated point and made our slow way homeward. The crew could scarcely pull a blade through the water; and they were perhaps already aware that their best efforts had been betrayed. They wanted to stop and rest: I was convinced that it would be easier to do it all in one effort, rather than to sit about drifting back the way we had come. Thus we limped back to the boathouse defeated, humiliated, out of sympathy with each other and the whole sport.

My father, it transpired, had watched the race from the Blue Anchor. No one could say that wasn't a good call.

I had been offered a clear shot at sporting glory and I had bogged it. I knew at the time that this wasn't just because I had made a mistake. There was a much deeper malaise. The fact was I was no bloody good. It wasn't just the business about looking for my father, and nor would it have been any better if I'd spotted him up there on the bridge cheering me on as if *Blue Peter*, as if the BBC, as if all television, were a secondary matter compared to my aspirations. I just wasn't a very good cox: not very good at command, not very good at manoeuvring, not very good at steering, not very good at race management or even the most basic of racing tactics. The business of my father showed how easily I could be distracted: but distraction wasn't the worst thing about the day. When it came to racing I was found wanting.

It wasn't that it didn't matter, it wasn't that it mattered too much. It was just that I failed to seize the moment when it was offered. Perhaps I was too concerned with my own insecurities, my own fears, than with the goal: and that's a crippling error at every level of sport.

And I was beginning to grasp something else. I had gone into the sport of rowing not in search of boats and water and speed, but in search of glory, or at least competence. And that really wasn't enough. I didn't love my sport at all. Not for its own sake. And this was a serious shortcoming. Sport has to begin in love.

# Chapter 13

# Oedipal Ping-pong

I slew my father. At last. My forehand loop found its range almost from the start and I won in straight sets. It was an occasion of long threatening. It happened in a disused chapel, for that was the place in Cornwall where the ping-pong table stood. It was, like the crossroads in the Oedipus myth, a sinister place. It was perhaps 300 years old and constructed with vast slabs of granite, the place where the community of tin-miners – the old engine house still stands on the cliff's summit a couple of hundred yards away from the chapel – took what comfort they could in the bleak words of the preachers and the Lord.

But when I was there the chapel was sacred to the revels of youth, ruled by a self-elected band deeply keen on exclusivity. It was a place of resentments, bad vibes and hyperawareness of male dominance hierarchies. It was a melancholy spot, and perhaps an appropriate stage for this apocalyptic event.

The table stood in plenty of space, and gave no favours to those with local knowledge. It offered a very fair test. I was in hard training, for I was playing several matches a day, even if I lost far more than I should. My father would take a fortnight off for these annual Cornish holidays.

Every year, then, it was inevitable that at some stage he and I would play our singles match. Naturally, over time these matches had grown a good deal closer. They had also grown less frequent. The table at home was not used nearly as often. John Murtagh and I seldom played these days. There had been no falling-out, simply a shift in the emphasis of our lives. And so it was in Cornwall that the game of Oedipal ping-pong was doomed to take place: the great forces that drive the world of heroes made it clear that there was no escaping our destiny.

The scores may have got closer but my father always had the edge. The rallies would be hard-fought. My loop and his blade-down super-scoop would duel for the mastery, and if my cross-court blaster was unplayable, I wouldn't often get a bat on his net-scraping down-the-liner. He would always win by the odd couple of points. All the same, eventually I began to take the occasional set off him. By then I was playing better in just about every facet of the game. I seemed to have all the requisite skills save that of scoring the last point of the match.

It was then I began to understand that matches do not only take place on the arena designated. They are also played around the breakfast table, with a row about late-night disturbance; they are played in long car journeys when the family tensions ball up; and they are played up and down the course of history.

Wrestling with your dad is one of the great archetypal situations; it's also one of the great images of helplessness. In this intimate situation the child is using all his strength, in the certainty that he can never prevail, while the father uses just a little of his own strength, in the certainty that he has more than enough to spare. It is a situation of great certainty, one of profound security, also of profound trust. But even in the safety of the struggle every father knows that the day will come when the balance will change. The way each father deals with that situation when it comes along is one of those complex personal frontiers.

So my father and I attempted to work out our lives and the subtle shifts of the dominance hierarchy to which we belonged, and we did so with ping-pong bats.

My day came at last, my loop landing on the table more or less at will, my father's play acquiring an unfamiliar ring of self-doubt, the blade-down slam now played in altogether inappropriate circumstances, hit with all the usual force but failing to come down and kiss the table. He was rattled; he sensed the momentousness of the occasion. I throttled back, a killer instinct for once taking me over. I eased up on the loops, keeping the ball in play, inviting the errors and the errors came. I offered him the opportunity to burst through the kitchen door and he did so, bringing down the ceiling with him. There was no doubt about it: I was the best ping-pong player in our family. I was champion of our house.

But the ping-pong table was not where our real battles took place. Ping-pong was not the enactment of the great and ancient familial battle in sporting form. No: these took place in other areas of family life. Our ping-pong matches were a time of relief: an outbreak of friendliness: an expression of intimacy. We didn't play ping-pong when we were on bad terms: we played when we were on good terms. My victory did not estrange me: on the contrary, it brought us closer. There were plenty of ways I could seek estrangement: very few, in what constituted our vocabulary back then, to establish – or re-establish – closeness. Though it has to be said here that we went on to find them.

This is one of the aspects of sport that can be forgotten. Sport is not a continuation of war: it's a truce. Sport can't be played in wholly hostile circumstances: there has to be measure of agreement. No matter how bitter a sporting encounter can be, no sport can take place unless the participants accept that this is not war but peace, not hostility but a kind of intimacy. It is sport's great contradiction: it is an act of peace cunningly disguised as a metaphor of battle and duel.

It's a fool who takes sport literally. If you attend an international rugby union match at Twickenham you will be startled by the public reverence given to the armed forces; last time I was there they fired off a field gun as part of the preliminaries. Wrong, all wrong. Guns are designed to kill people. Sport is designed as an activity you walk away from. Sport is not among the arts of war: it's one of the arts of peace, as the story of the informal Christmas Day truce with its pick-up football match in no-man's-land makes clear.

Ping-pong represented a kind of no-man's-land in the complex dealings – by no means all warfare and hostility – between my father and myself. So did all sport: discussion of cricket, watching cricket together on the television, watching rugby, for that matter, especially rugby league, when it was Wigan playing. These were things we shared: to which we turned with relief. Sport's hostilities provided us with a place in which we could set our own futile and temporary hostilities to one side.

All the same, I did win that match, and I won most of the matches we played afterwards. Nor was it just the power and occasional accuracy of my forehand loop that made the difference in this long-running sporting series. I had the upper hand now: at least in ping-pong. And if this was not something to presume on, it was certainly an indication that life was not so much changing as opening up. It wasn't about beating my father; that it was just a station on the way. It was about making my own decisions. It wasn't as safe a prospect as wrestling with your dad, but not without its meaning.

# Chapter 14

# Faster Than You'll Ever Live to Be

Mr Tasker was, even by the standards of my schoolmasters, notable for his reluctance to take on unnecessary work. So it occurred to him that the best place to conduct the weekly gym lesson for his fifth-form class was the staff room. He left us to it, and a very good plan it was too. Thus the Tossers – a self-applauding band of half a dozen who all went on to become prefects – went off to play Eton Fives among themselves; three or four would quietly slip away and get on with whatever they wanted to get on with, and the rest of us would play ferocious games of five-a-side football.

We would stick with the same teams from one week to another; none of your gym-masterly pick-up rituals before each session, so there was every opportunity for resentments and rivalries to build up. And we went at it hammer and tongs. My team centred on Ian and Stuart, great mates of mine and very decent players. Quite often we were the best team of the week. Mostly I was goalie. I got to make plenty of saves: it was a small space and we played with few inhibitions, so the ball spent a lot of time ricocheting about. The noise was colossal: echoing shouts of encouragement, instruction and recrimination, great slamming impacts of ball against foot, against wall, against wall bar, against the piled-up 'forms' that we used as goals. These were wooden benches that had multiple uses in the gym: I had balanced on them, leapt from them and climbed them many times. Now they were goals. We had to use them because there were no proper goals with nets. Obviously. I mean, that might encourage an interest in association football, might it not?

By this time I was starting to catch up with the rest in terms of size, without compromising my quickness and agility, so I did OK. Not great but OK. And, as we played, I began to discover something I had never really known in sport. It was a deeply intoxicating thing. It was as if I had cracked the secret not just of goalkeeping, not just of football, but of sport itself. For the first time I was taking part in a confrontational sport at Emanuel School with a sense of delight. This came from something very specific, though it's a little elusive of explanation.

It was the ability to be a step – half a step – less than that, maybe a quarter of a step – ahead of the game. That was a tiny amount but one that made all the difference. Down in my crouch, always watching the ball, always watching the feet, there were times when I could see exactly what was going on – *a fraction of a second before it actually happened*. Nothing mystical about this: it was a matter of angles and body shapes. But I could see the ball as the foot came down to strike it, and I would know where the ball was going and where I had to be to stop it: the bass thump of a well-struck shot, followed not by the detonation of ball against form but by the softer stinging slap of ball against palm: a save I knew I was going to make very slightly before the ball was struck.

This was not exactly infallible, but there were occasions when I could pull off a decent save, and, in a way, that was enough, just as a single devastating forehand loop was pleasure enough in any game of ping-pong, no matter what the result. But I was part of a team, and I wanted my skills, such as they were, to be part of a wider, shared, corporate effort, so the question of winning and losing was not without its relevance.

I still have a vivid memory of the goalie's view of the action: precociously hairy legs and grubby white plimsolls – no trainers in those days – and always the damn ball. The erratic course it would take, the dark wood of the wall bars; and the way the ball would fly from those oncoming feet in my direction, sometimes to beat me, yes of course, quite often to beat me, but sometimes not. Sometimes it seemed that the ball could never get past me, I was reading the patterns of those feet so clearly. Sometimes as I lunged and extended a hand, it seemed to me that my hand was attracting the ball, rather than the other way around: as if the forward were somehow complicit with the goalkeeper in creating this spectacle of the saved shot.

It was a revelation. I had been privileged to experience sport, for a few moments at a time, as real ball players do. Some years later I read about the same phenomenon in one of the Modesty Blaise thrillers, *The Impossible Virgin*. Modesty has been persuaded to explain her concept of *muga*. 'There's *muga* in any form of close combat,' she says. 'It just means short-circuiting the mind so you react subconsciously, but with exactly the right move ... Someone comes at you, and you take in a dozen things about their attitude – speed, balance, intent, committal, posture and so on. And everything's changing every split second, so there's virtually a graph curve for every item. It's much too quick for conscious thought. You need to develop an instantaneous computer so you can feed in all the data and come up with the right counter. When you do get it right, the counter just flows. It's inevitable, so inevitable that it can sometimes look as if the opponent cooperated in throwing himself, or whatever it is that happens to him. The instantaneous computer, that's *muga*.'

It sounds mystical but it isn't. You can put it in highfalutin terms, but it's a very simple principle. It's very complex in practice though: increasingly complex the higher the level of sport at which you observe it. Thus you can watch Roger Federer play three successive strokes, drawing an opponent out of position and then upping the pace and intensity with the kill shot: and, yes, it really does look as if the opponent has cooperated in his own demise. Or you can watch Lionel Messi slalom through a defence, and it seems that he is fractionally ahead of those trying to stop him, that he has the priceless advantage of having read the script. Top performers at the peak of their game can sometimes look like exam-room cheats: as if they had seen the paper before they came in, knew what questions they were going to be asked and prepared themselves accordingly.

Cobb, through on goal again. Big lad, forthright attitude. Nothing subtle about Cobb. Right-footed: a blaster, not a placer. So he'll kick across his body in the usual way, putting the ball to his left, my right. He's not that accurate, so look out for mishits. Come on, Cobb: I'm way ahead of you. As Clint said in *High Plains Drifter*, I'm faster than you'll ever live to be. Crack! and the ball is struck as sweetly as Cobb can strike it, and it's not bad but it's not great and anyway I'm there, not even at full stretch, a hand on it that was there in advance, attracting the ball's impact and there was Stuart to clear up and pass along the wall bars to Ian. So let's say Ian scored and we won again, because no one can contradict me now, certainly not Cobb.

And because of those lowly encounters I understand – not with my mind and my intellect, but with my sporting guts – what it's like to play sport with the full power of *muga*, the sporting computer: to play with that mixture of observation, understanding and anticipation. There's a sense of withdrawal here: of being slightly detached from the action: as if you're going through a series of movements long premeditated. I, too, have sampled one of sport's most intoxicating drinks: supped from the chalice *muga*. Just as I've seen a kestrel and known how Gerard Manley Hopkins feels, just as I loved Christine Hill and knew how Romeo felt, so I beat Cobb when he was clean through – and so I know how Federer and Messi felt.

# Chapter 15

# The Graveyard of Sport

It was at the Greg Hunt Memorial Piss-up that Brian Murphy, former stroke of Junior A and latterly Colts A, Dick Bradburn, who rowed seven in the same boats, and I sat down to discuss the vexed question of how many bridges I had actually struck during my career as a cox. Brian had become a successful barrister; Dick had pursued an adventurous career in Eastern Europe. So we put our minds to the task and we seemed to recall a certain difference of opinion with Putney Railway Bridge. Certainly there was the rather more terrible incident at Kew, though it was an advancing crew rather than the bridge that took the full force of the impact. But no, I insisted. I never struck Barnes Bridge. What I struck was a boat that had dragged its mooring and was very close to Barnes Bridge.

Oh dear. There really were rather too many disasters. I had run aground in a heavy clinker-built eight called *Old Subtlety*, though that could be regarded as a misfortune. There were other incidents of notable incompetence, however, and they began to stack up. By this time we were being coached by a rather ineffectual teacher whose name has gone from me. So let's call him Mr Carter. It was his ineffectiveness that set in train the series of incidents that led to the Barnes Bridge disaster.

We were rowing in fairly fierce conditions; copious draughts of land water had made this as rapid an ebb tide as I'd ever experienced. We crawled our way upstream, against its flow, for as far as seemed sensible, hugging the shore where the stream is at its slowest. The rules of the river state that when you travel against the tide you keep to the inside, and when you go with the tide you take the fullest possible advantage of it by rowing in the middle. Then Mr Carter told us to turn, a manoeuvre that took us some way ahead of him. We could hear him in the distance yelling through his megaphone, telling us to travel with the tide, paddling firm, until further notice. This was a little naïve of him.

So we set off from Kew Bridge and hit a very fair rhythm: this lot had the makings of a pretty decent crew, remember. There's a fine feeling when a boat starts to move: that power balanced on a knife edge, in the manner of the dressage horse. Yes, even we shared the feeling experienced by Matthew Pinsent and his gold medal-winning crew. I loved the long glide, no need to hurry, slide forward almost languorously as Brian set the pace; at this stage of the stroke you go faster by not rowing than by rowing. Then the strike: another lurching leap of power followed by another long graceful glide. In fine shape we shot Chiswick Bridge and rowed on past the brewery, Barnes Bridge up ahead.

'Where the hell's bloody Carter?'

'Perhaps we should wait for him.'

'Suppose so … easy all!' And we stopped and I looked back over my shoulder but no coach was in sight. We seemed to have burned him off completely, silly sod. Perhaps I'd better take the crew back into the boathouse, just the other side of the bridge. A bit irregular, but then it was a bit irregular to leave your coach back in Chiswick. I looked back again. Decided it was time to make a decision. Looked forward.

It was then I realised that we were almost on top of a sizeable motor launch. It was still attached to its mooring but it had shifted under the force of all this water to the middle of the stream. Our own speed, coupled with that of the outrushing tide, had caused me to misjudge distance. We were lined up skew-whiff half across the stream now, at something close to 45 degrees. I rammed the steering line hard left, implored the crew to row away. I'd have done better to get a couple of decent strokes from two and four to straighten us up, but it's rather too late to realise that now. So we rammed the damn motorboat: rammed it damn hard, and it was Dick's rigger that took the full force, bending it out of shape, rendering it useless. We disentangled ourselves and limped home under the power of the bow four, and then it was explanation time.

It was then I realised that my love of coxing had turned into a deep hatred and an enduring misery. It was so very cold in winter. It was so very demoralising being a passenger. And, to make it worse, I was very bad indeed at the few things a cox is supposed to do. I was bored stupid for most of it and useless in a crisis. As soldiering is said to be 99 per cent boredom and 1 per cent terror, so coxing had become for me. I was trapped in a loveless cycle of sport. Of course, I tried to hide from the awkward truth, but each time I fitted myself on to that narrow little shelf at the back of the boat I felt a small thud of despair. I hoped not for excellence but for the avoidance of disaster.

Such circumstances, as I learned soon enough, made disaster inevitable. The final, fatal collision came at Kew Railway Bridge. The river was lower than I'd ever seen it, and I wasn't confident I could get through the inside arch without running aground. I asked Mr Carter: he suggested, logically enough, that I try the centre arch – against the rules of the river but there seemed no option. So I pulled out towards the middle of the stream and got inextricably entangled with an eight that was coming the other way at a fair lick. I hadn't seen it at all. Coxing, by definition, is about coping with an immense blind spot, for you have eight people, all bigger than you, bang in front. This second boat had been completely concealed from me by the pillars of the bridge and by my crew. No excuse: I should have made doubly and trebly sure of what was going on before attempting this unconventional manoeuvre. It was at this point, completely entangled with another boat, that my brain froze. I could go neither forward nor back, I couldn't think of a single order or manoeuvre that would reduce the scale of this disaster. The crew so horrifically caught up with us was, I think, the Junior A, a year younger than us, but with a cox – Nick O'Keefe, his name comes singing back on the floodtide of memory – infinitely more self-certain in the art of coxswainship. So I suffered the ultimate humiliation of being told what to do by O'Keefe. We managed to separate ourselves and proceed. Carter, cravenly, placed the blame on me. All of it. 'I didn't mean go that far towards the centre of the stream.' Yeah, right, thanks. But it was still my cock-up more than anyone else's, and the next time I went to the boathouse I was formally relieved of my command, told that I was never going to make a cox. It was a fair call, inevitable, and I accepted it with resignation, without protest.

As it happens, this wasn't the worst error made by a cox on the Tideway. That came at the Boat Race of 1984, when the Cambridge cox, Peter Hobson, was taking his crew through a pre-race warm-up. And he rammed a barge full on. The beautiful canary-yellow boat came back to the boathouse at Putney with its bow bent upwards at 45 degrees. It wasn't the first time he had done such a thing. In the crew biographies in the Boat Race official programme he had listed among his interests 'barge re-shaping'. I was there on the hard as he courageously faced the press and explained: 'It was in my blind spot.' One hell of a blind spot, people commented. But I, more than anyone else reporting the Boat Race that day, knew how he felt. He rose above it, so he must have been a tough-minded fellow, and went on to cox internationally. I didn't.

That moment when I stepped from the boat after our adventures at Kew Railway Bridge was the last time in my life that I took part in sport because I had to. Though it required a fair level of deviousness to reach such a point, I was never again ordered to take part in sport at Emanuel School. From now on I would only ever be a volunteer; and, to be frank, I had no great idea of ever volunteering. It seemed that sport and I had finally fallen out. The Kew Entanglement was the death of just one more sporting dream: there was now a veritable graveyard in my mind commemorating such deaths. The death of cricket was an ornate and extravagant tomb of the kind you find in an Italian cemetery, with fulsome inscriptions and weeping angels, while others, like the death of running, were more sober and functional. The death of rowing came somewhere in between: mourned not for what the sport had become for me, but for what it had been when I set out in the hope of becoming the small but excellent dynamic force that led Emanuel to their inevitable victory in the Schools Head of the River on the Tideway and in the Princess Elizabeth Cup at Henley.

The attentive reader will have noticed at this point that the most important matter on the sporting agenda was Blagdons avoidance. In theory – and not allowing for my deviousness – if I left the Boat Club I would be expected once again to make that soul-killing journey to New Malden. So, affecting a sense of keenness and a love of the Boat Club that I didn't really possess, I offered to take on the job of school boatman: to conduct the crews in and out of the river on Wednesday afternoons and Saturday mornings. A little touched, I think, by this – resigned or blind to my hypocrisy – they accepted. I took on the job with my dear and unathletic friend John Kent. We did it together for a fair while, gradually putting in all sorts of little improvements. For example, before we started on Wednesday afternoon we would visit the Coach and Horses in Barnes High Street. We tried other pubs. After a while, we started trying out the pubs of Streatham, so on Saturday mornings we met at the Leigham Arms rather than a riverside pub: better again. At one point John invited me to join him at a youth club he attended. It was a pretty ghastly place, as you'd expect, but it was here that I met Christine Hill.

If someone had told me then that I would never play sport again, I would have received the news with a cheery nod. My urge to prove myself by means of sport was gone. It was literature and the idea of being a writer that now filled my soul: I had just started reading James Joyce and his dreams of artistry had become my own. Besides, I was no longer the smallest boy in my class. I was catching up. I was filled with dreams of words and wild and inaccurate thoughts about girls. Sport had failed me as I had failed sport, but these failures could be set aside with other things I had struggled with and forgotten: maths, chemistry, physics, Russian, Latin. From now on I would do the things I wanted to do: the things I was able to do. *Non serviam!* Stephen's soul's cry in *A Portrait of the Artist as a Young Man* was now mine. Sport was just one of those nets that I resolved to fly by: *non ludam!* I will not play!

One last Boat Club moment. John and I had gone straight to the boathouse for once, but for some reason we found ourselves carrying straight on, in defiance of some odd looks and a couple of questioning calls. We walked the length of Duke's Meadow and eventually reached the Dove. Recklessly, we took our pints outside and stood there drinking and looking out over the river: fine sport, I'm sure you'll agree. At one point a launch backed in and held position just underneath us. John and I were too much involved in conversation to appreciate what was going on until we became aware that a couple of heads had turned and were now looking up at us from the launch. The launch was the *Colonel Charles*, its crew our own schoolmasters. 'Barnes! Kent!'

We raised our glasses to them. What else could we do? They pulled out. Nothing further was said on the matter: and if I have been short of praise for some aspects of the school in these pages, let me stop for a moment and praise its sense of tolerance. Within a year I was to push that tolerance to the limit but it remained in place. The school song, three verses of outrageous pomposity and pretension, was even then a standing joke and an embarrassment even to the school's true patriots. Its first line was, and is: 'Emanuel! For the noble aim …'

If tolerance is the noble aim, the school did a fair job.

# Chapter 16

# Sport is Bourgeois

So I became an intellectual dissident: an official school rebel, with long hair, daring deviations from school uniform (grey suede boots, red PVC mac) and attitudes to match, flirting hard with radical politics and eager to see the world in a new way. Those who were actually about in the sixties know that this was a time of bitter opposition. The attempt to silence dissident and inconvenient voices was seen as a crusade. The Tossers, now all prefects, believed that the Establishment – crucial word of the time – was by definition right. Those who disagreed were not mistaken: they were morally at fault. There was no debate: there couldn't be. Questioning authority was wrong: end of discussion.

Oddly enough, this is a non-debate that still continues in sport, especially football. One of the moral lessons sport is supposed to teach is respect for authority. The umpire is always right. The referee must never be questioned. Football has consistently refused to take on available technologies to help in decision-making: the referee's authority is more important than the correctness of his decisions. Other sports have gradually and reluctantly gone the other way: no sport has gone to the dogs as a result.

The Tossers and the Establishment believed that sport was an important thing. They believed that sport taught the need for conformity as well as the importance of authority. This gave me a moral obligation to despise sport. There seemed no escape. So sport was bourgeois. So was practically everything else.

Bourgeois: few words have given me such joy. I could use it in conversation with my father and it was a forehand loop that never missed the table. So if I was to achieve any kind of consistency, I had to hate sport. Those too deeply committed to the sporting life we called 'Bruisers'. It was a derisive term. Truth lay in literature, the visual arts, music, imagination, freedom, higher moral values and in working for a better and a fairer society. In opposition to these lofty aims were philistinism, oppression, plonking literalism, power-seeking, hypocrisy and sport.

I tried really quite hard to despise sport but I never made a good job of it. My heart wasn't in it. This was because, for all my intellectual posturing, sport was still capable of firing my imagination, every bit as much as the works of Joyce and T. S. Eliot. Prufrock, Stephen, Bloom, Molly, Tiresias, Sweeny: yes indeed, but also there was Muhammad Ali, Billie-Jean King, George Best, Garry Sobers, Bob Beamon, Tommie Smith. I really couldn't maintain the notion that they were acting out a triviality for the bourgeoisie in order to promote bourgeois values and inhibit revolutionary consciousness in the oppressed: not when Ali renounced his 'slave-name' of Cassius Clay, when Billie-Jean introduced the troubling notions of feminism, when Best stood for freedom of genius in an oppressive world, when Sobers and Beamon redefined the thing they did and Smith stood up for the rights of the oppressed even on the Olympic podium.

Why should the devil have all the good tunes? And why should the forces of oppression have all the fun: what right had they to sport?

The right wing has always tried to hijack sport for its own purposes, but sport has never played along. The right-wingers try to control sport and always they find that sport is too big. Hitler had to face that problem at the Berlin Olympic Games of 1936. Authoritarian figures control sport much as they herd cats. You can assemble a team of short-haired, disciplined, well-organised and united footballers: and then you have Best dancing through them, making each of the opposition – but most especially their boss, manager or leader – look a fool. Sport is bigger than the people who seek to control it for their own purposes. Sport can never be the monopoly of a certain view of humankind: both sport and sport's performers are too various. Too human.

So I despised the Emanuel boys who played in the first XI and the first XV and the first VIII, and yet I thrilled to the great sporting events: Best and Manchester United in the European Cup, the Olympic Games in Mexico City in 1968, the visit of the West Indian cricket team in 1966, when they won the Test series 3–1. I opposed any hint of cosying up to South Africa in the D'Oliveira affair and knew it was right that the tour was called off. I supported the people who disrupted matches involving the South African rugby team, but it was clear that sport was not to blame for injustice. The forces of injustice, throughout the history of sport, have tried to recruit sport to their cause and, time and again, sport has triumphantly failed them. I saw such things at first hand when I attended the Olympic Games, and this brings us back to the great Chinese female divers I saw at their work. Rebellious temperaments like Fu Mingxia and Guo Jingjing were too good to be dropped, too strong to be silenced: standing up for rampant individuality in the face of a government that valued conformity.

And there was something else that survived my time as sport's intellectual dissident and survived the near-total failure of my schoolboy sporting ambitions. It was the absurd persistence of my daydream of sport. For all that I resolutely and gratefully turned my back on sport, there was, buried deep, never mentioned and never examined, my hope of playing sport again. Only properly.

It was nothing like my fantasies of being a schoolboy champion of the world on Streatham Common. It was a vision of movement: a kind of psychokinetic precognition. I foresaw myself in motion, doing something half right: movements in which I felt committed, agile, controlled, accurate: almost graceful.

I no longer wanted to be champion of the world – or at least I accepted that was never going to be – but I still had inside me the notion of being champion of the moment, king of the unforgiving minute. I saw myself taking part in sport and, however briefly, doing it right. Not for the applause, or for the approval of my team-mates, though such things would prove to be fairly enjoyable, but for the sense of moving. Knowing that, when put to the test, I could sometimes be almost competent.

Not as a justification for my existence, nothing as footling. Such things would come from family and writing and the cause I adopted. I never needed sport to justify my existence: rather, to enhance it: to make life more vivid. Ever so slightly more meaningful. That daydream, adapted from Streatham Common, Sunnyhill School and the Cubs and put through the mill at Emanuel, refused to go away. It persisted for ten years buried beneath the thousand matters that crop up in that fearsome decade that lies between the comparatively safe havens of late teens and late 20s.

And it was then that I found myself facing fearsome obstacles and an audience of a couple of hundred, with hope and terror fighting for the mastery. Who'd have thought it?

Part Two

# Supernova

Period of Maximum
Brightness

# Chapter 17

# Elimination

Picture your political dissident and intellectual despiser of sport a decade later. Wearing a tie of all things: what new and dreadful madness is this? Not just a tie: a neat jacket, a black velvet-covered cap, jodhpurs and riding boots that reached my knees. And sitting on a horse. Obviously.

Or perhaps not terribly obviously, but there it is. I had caught the horsey bug, and, as I seldom weary of saying, it's like Catholicism or measles: relatively trivial when encountered in childhood, infinitely more serious when caught as a grown-up. I was in all this fancy gear because I was making a return to sport. I was entering competition again. And I was terrified.

I was so strung up that I found a curious lag between the decision to perform a routine physical action and the ability to do it; as if something was interfering with the messages from my brain to my limbs. My voice had gone slightly peculiar too: certainly it didn't sound like my own. I felt as if I was being gently throttled. But this sense of funk was accompanied by a sensation of enthralment. I couldn't wait to see what happened next. I wanted to perform the task that lay before me, but I also wanted not to do it. Right then it was a narrow thing, about 60:40 in favour of kicking on. I always felt that terrible contradiction, though in different proportions. It's a universal thing: part of all sport and doubly so for sports that have a bit of physical risk in them.

The place was Beas River, in what were then called the New Territories of Hong Kong. I had gone to Hong Kong after four glorious hippified years in and around Bristol University and four rather more circumscribed years on local papers. I really ought to have been treading the road that leads towards Fleet Street but instead I took the side turning that led to adventure.

Horses weren't supposed to be a part of it, but I went up to the New Territories for a pleasure ride and discovered that the only horses available were ex-racehorses, and that they took a bit more riding than the riding-school horses I had sat on in the past. I took a heavy fall at an inadvertent and immoderate gallop from a stunning chestnut named Sirius and got up inspired. I wanted to do this all over again but without the fall.

And so I got serious. I took lessons, learned to ride – as opposed to just sitting there – and then I learned to jump. I acquired a delightful schoolmistress of a mare named Favour on a kind of lease-hire basis and soon I was being asked when I was going to start competing.

I resisted hard and successfully for quite a while. I insisted that I was in it for the horses and the pure joy of horsemanship, that I had no wish to be judged. Bit by bit my objections were broken down. I didn't want to dress up like this, I didn't want people to watch me ride, I didn't want to make a fool of myself in public. But the idea of taking a serious course of jumps in a big open space thrilled me, and I wanted to see if I could do it. Because I was pretty certain I could. I wanted to test myself, but not against other people. That was just part of the deal.

Beas River is part of the Hong Kong Jockey Club, and its proceedings tend to be formal and formidable. The equestrian events at the Beijing Olympic Games of 2008 were held at Beas River. When I arrived a little less than 30 years earlier for a somewhat lesser competition I was out of my depth from the moment I arrived. For a start my friends were all unrecognisable in riding jackets, stocks, ties, white jods, often also with overdone make-up and overwrought nerves.

I felt horribly out of place. I had no idea what to do: what the protocol was, what you did about warming up, what you did about walking the course, what you did about waiting your turn, what you did about greeting the judges when you entered the ring. I knew what you had to do after that – jump the bloody fences – but that was the least of my worries.

I had chosen to enter a competition called Take Your Own Line; you were allowed to take any fence in any order, the bigger fences counting for more points. It was a competition designed for experienced riders, a fun event after the more serious stuff had been finished. It was a ludicrous event for a novice rider to attempt.

Like a hobbledehoy at a banquet I kept a close look at what everyone else was doing, though it wasn't a matter of which knife and fork to use, more a matter of what you did while sitting on a horse. At the very last moment I noticed that gentlemen remove their hats when they salute the judges: I had been planning to do so with a mere bow, girly fashion. But what happened next was much worse.

I walked Favour into the ring with my mouth tasting as if I had spent the last hour sucking pennies. I could feel her jogging excitedly beneath me: she was keyed up, ready to rumble. She knew about shows. She was a different horse from the one I knew in practice and training, but not that much different. Just Favour-plus: and that seemed to be a good thing to me. I made my salute, got my hat back on all right, and asked her to canter a circle. Astonishing. At home I'd have had to administer a nudge with my heels: here in the stress of competition I thought canter and she cantered. Competition inspires. Competition brings out your best, that's one of the reasons why we do it. Favour was responding to the task ahead rather than the prospect of victory, but she too felt the excitement of being put to the test: at facing a thrillingly demanding task. Her appetite for the job fuelled my own. This was good. This was better than good.

I brought her on a good line towards the first fence, just as I'd been taught, just as I'd practised. And – savour the miracle – we jumped it. We jumped it neatly, competently, perhaps even stylishly. I still have a photograph somewhere of that historic event. We're halfway over: she's stretching out like a good 'un. I am lunging up her neck, in a good balance. My hands are too far forward and my reins much too long, but she was always a very forgiving mare. And damn it: we were flying, we were over the jump. My first competitive action on horseback and –

BONG!

Elimination. I was baffled. I rode out of the ring wondering what could possibly have gone wrong. Someone told me I had failed to ride through the start. 'I didn't know there was a start you had to ride through,' I said.

Apparently there were a pair of markers that you had to ride through on your way to the first fence. Perhaps someone should have told me. Perhaps I should have made a point of finding out. My journey to Beas River took three and a half hours from my home on Lamma Island. So that was seven hours of travel for one small jump and one rather large lesson. Part of me thought I should have been let off, allowed to start again, poor chap, it's not his fault. But if sport doesn't take itself seriously it isn't really sport. Just messing about.

Years later I was covering the Atlanta Olympic Games of 1996 when Bettina Hoy made the exact opposite error to me. She went through the start twice. This was in the showjumping segment of the three-day event. She rode through the start, the clock started and then she cantered a solemn circle before going through the start for a second time. What possessed her? A brainstorm. She got herself lost: perhaps in space, perhaps in time, perhaps both. She then rode a lovely round and thought that she had won the individual gold medal for herself and the team gold medal for Germany, but she was later demoted and given 14 time penalties, incurred while she was circling round to make her second pass through the start. There was a protest, a counter-protest, it went to the Court for Arbitration in Sport and Bettina and Germany lost amid great unhappiness and lasting bitterness. And I have every sympathy for her. And no sympathy at all.

I sympathised with a person who could make such a stupid mistake at the most important moment of her life: the moment for which all other moments had been a preparation. But I deserved my elimination at the Jockey Club Show and she deserved her time penalties at the Olympic Games. Sport is an artificial world. It is created from a shared illusion draped over a rickety framework of rules and conventions. Without those rules sport has no structure, no meaning, no existence.

It's not rules for the sake of rules. It's not about blind obedience to unseen authority as the right-wingers like to believe. It's just that sport can't stand up without its scaffolding of rules. It's not a free-for-all: even the scruffiest of kickabouts requires agreement on what you can and cannot do. Sport must always be, to some degree, formal. And of course, formidable.

I thought at the time that the decision to eliminate me at Beas River was mean-spirited, petty-minded and cruel. And so it was. Sport's like that. Sport has to be like that or it has no meaning. It has to be a world without much room for compassion or understanding. Cruelty is essential to its existence. I remember in the playground at Sunnyhill School we sought to mitigate the cruelties of sport with the not-included rule. You couldn't be out the first ball you faced: no, that was too cruel. 'First ball not included!' the victim would implore, and, for the most part, the bowlers and fielders agreed. To be out first ball was too cruel a thing for even our enemies.

But sport – proper sport – needs such suffering. Without cruelty there is no sport.

And I, cruelly done by, could only blame my own folly. And I would be back. Something about the formal perils of horsey competition had taken hold of me, and I longed in my soul to get back: to feel the same terror, to turn that terror into action, and to jump, jump, jump. To fly.

# Chapter 18

# A Good Start

A couple of weeks later I entered the Novice Rider showjumping competition at Lo Wu Saddle Club. It was the first event of the day, beginning at eight o'clock. I was still working out how to do this by public transport when Liz said she would make sure I got there on time. This was something of a surprise. Liz ran Dragon Hall in those days and she wasn't altogether easy to deal with. It's possible that Dragon Hall's majestic owner, Helen Wu, had spoken to her: she would not have been impressed when one of her riders confessed that he didn't know that you had to go through a start before you rode a round of showjumping. But it's possible that Liz decided to put things right herself.

Either way, she put her heart into doing so, and that was a fine thing.

I arrived at Liz's flat the night before; her husband was in some suited expat job with a flat included in the deal. He put up with this invasion good-humouredly enough and even gave me a beer. I slept in the spare room; Liz woke me a little before five. She drove me through the New Territories to Dragon Hall, and on the way she talked me through the protocol in great detail. She told me the best way to ride a showjumping round in competition and what I should do if I went clear. We arrived and, after Favour was tacked up, she bandaged her legs: a now-outmoded and desperately fiddly practice designed to protect the horse's tendons, which come under stress when jumping.

I was still gut-wrenchingly nervous, but I was aware that the nature of this condition was subtly different this time around. I wasn't so much concerned with the sort of show I would make as with the fences I would have to jump. This was some kind of advance. As I hacked over to Lo Wu it was very clear to me that I wanted to get out there and jump fences. If Lo Wu had fallen through the earth's crust and the show was cancelled, I wouldn't have been pleased. There was still a touch of funk in my fear, of course there was: but this time it was funk made functional. I was altogether without the hint of paralysis

I had known at Beas River. I wanted to jump. This is part of what sport means: making your fear work for you: making an ally, not an enemy of funk. You need that sense of funk: but in the right proportions – this was more like 80:20 – and then converted into ambition. That is sport's alchemy – to turn the base metal of fear into the gold of competitive competence.

I walked the course. It was not the question of related distance that bothered me, even though that's the key to all showjumping. It was the challenging – at least to me – task of jumping the right fences in the right order. I didn't want to do a Wandsworth Common this morning. No short cuts. Almost as importantly, if I knew which fence came next I would be able to set off from the fence before on the right line: taking an easy, rhythmic, cantering curve that became a straight line three or four paces from the fence. I had done this sort of thing in practice again and again: now I wanted to do it over a full course of jumps in a large open space. I wanted to do it under the stresses of sport. I wanted to be tested: not so much to see if I could win, but to see if I could do it.

After that I warmed up. Practice rings are horrible places, jangling with other people's neuroses. Many obsessively jump the practice fences, some apparently in the middle of a full-scale jumping lesson: a worthy notion but a bit late in the day. I preferred – and always did – to work mostly on the flat, looking for suppleness, responsiveness, relaxation, impulsion, getting the horse to work in curves, bending the body. That's the difference between racing and the equestrian disciplines I was pursuing. You want more than straight lines. Above all, you want to engage the power behind the saddle, where the big jumping muscles are grouped. The balance is quite different.

The showground at Lo Wu is dead flat, open and rather bleak, but with a startling line of mountains a short distance away. There was a lot of space. I stood Favour and we watched the other competitors go, and I tried to remember the order of the jumps once again. Then I put her through a series of small, simple manoeuvres until our names were called. A moment of not-quite-vomity terror, and we were trotting into the ring. I saluted the judges in the proper fashion, just as I had practised, and then asked for canter. Favour, with her show-ring responsiveness, rolled forward at the mere thought and did so with immense delight, taking a real pleasure in her own movement. We circled once – but without going through the start – to get the feel of things, and then I committed us. This time through the start. That was a good start. Aim at the first fence. Clear it: and now look for the second, look now, as you land,

and I did that and Favour responded to my change in body shape and we were cantering smooth, easy, relaxed at fence two. Easy!

It was round about fence six of 12 that everything changed. Everything about the round: everything about the day: everything about my sporting life. I daren't look too far ahead, daren't think a single jump past the one that lay before us, but there was a great warm golden glow flowing through me: 'I can fucking do this!'

And I could. I felt a great sense of calm and purpose mixing itself up with my anxiety. The rest of the fences just flowed, one after the next, and Favour, who knew this game of old and had jumped at a much higher standard, gave me her wisdom and experience. When we cleared the last fence we still hadn't touched a pole. We landed. Then, even better, I remembered to ride through the finish. 'And that's a clear round for Simon Barnes and Favour.' Music of all music: the B Minor Mass and the Monteverdi Vespers and the Coronation Mass all rolled into one. Surely nothing could ever top that.

Or could it? I kept Favour warm and supple and then we were back in the ring for the jump-off. This time, speed mattered: fastest clear round wins it. But this was not the moment for heroics. I cut no corners, I stuck to our rhythmic ground-eating canter, and we went round in a leisurely but relentless way and were clear again. To my inexpressible delight that was good enough for fifth place. We lined up: rosettes were handed out all the way down to fifth. A kind lady tucked an orange ribbon into Favour's bridle and said: 'Well done.' Someone took a picture: my smile of thanks is ridiculous. Far too big. It would have been considered a mite excessive if I'd just won the Olympics. But I felt as if I'd done rather better than that: fifth place, an orange ribbon, a real reward handed out to a real horseman. The winner led us off in a fast showy-offy canter around the showground and Favour and I followed in our turn. I stood in the irons and leant over her neck in a great parade of exulting speed and even then we managed not to disgrace ourselves. It was as if we had cantered through a gateway into a new and beautiful and enthralling country. When I returned to the collecting ring, there was Liz with her nicest smile, patting her hands together in applause.

This was not just about being competent at sport. Being, in a small way, good at sport. It went deeper than that. More than anything else it was about the terrible horsey bug that had taken me over. I had discovered that I loved being with horses: now I had proved myself – in public – at a relatively demanding task. And I had loved it: well, love is too weak a word for the sense of compulsion, of total physical involvement in so joyous a task. There was the spice of physical danger; my fall from Sirius that first day at Dragon Hall had knocked what little sense I had from my head, certainly when it comes to horses.

The danger was intimately and mysteriously connected with the public nature of the sport: the performance side of things. I was setting myself out to be judged, by the formal rules and customs of sport, and by the gossip and observations of my fellow-competitors and the rest who attended these shows. Both were, in theory, alarming: both were, in practice, stimulating. By making yourself vulnerable, you gain something. It's possible that I rode better that morning than I had ever done in my life: a performance forced from me by the thrilling stresses of competition.

And that principle is at the heart of sport. Athletes don't set personal bests in practice. And yet, as I was to learn later, you can play superbly in the nets before a cricket match and still be out first ball. It's a contradiction at the heart of sport: competition takes away, but competition can also give you stuff you never thought you possessed.

# Chapter 19

# A Madman's Joy

A few months later I had established myself as a competent novice showjumper. I was capable of taking Favour round a modest course in a calm and accurate way, and that gave me incalculable joy. Then came a new challenge: the one I had set my heart on from the first moment I took a horse over a jump. The showjumping had been, as it were, a stalking horse for these much bigger ambitions: an audition for the real thing. Now, when the notice went up inviting entries to the Jockey Club's two-day event, I put my name down at once, knowing that this was both expected and approved. Favour and I were well up to this.

Eventing is the greatest equestrian discipline of them all. In some moods I will claim it as the great sporting discipline bar none. Rider and horse must be jack of all trades and master of one: the one in question being cross-country riding. That is to say, riding several miles over a course of solid obstacles, some of them inviting, some of them seriously alarming. I had always liked to be out in the country, always preferred this to riding and jumping in an arena. Gill, my first riding teacher at Dragon Hall, was a deeply understanding person and took this on, so that I learned the basics of riding and then of jumping out on the tracks of the steeply undulating countryside. I was thrilled by the idea of stringing all these jumps together with no need to worry about people and horses coming the other way.

I was also concerned. So I invented mental rehearsal. This, I was to learn some years later, is something that sports psychologists are keen on. You make an extended series of dry runs in your mind before you actually do it. Dick Fosbury, inventor of the once revolutionary Fosbury Flop, now the standard technique for the high-jump, would run through the jump in his mind several times before he moved. You could see that in his eyes and his lips: mouthing and eyeing an approach and a take-off. You don't just think: you aim to do the job, yes, psychokinetically. You need to feel the movement with your mind. That's what Dick did: that's what I did.

I wrote down the jumps in the order I would take them and, time and again, I would ride the course, no matter where I happened to be. There I was, on the ferry to Lamma, eyeing and mouthing as I rode the cross-country course at Beas River. As I came to each fence I could feel my hands clench around the rein of air: at this point I would take a pull and prepare for my approach: at this next point I would kick on: here I would move with some circumspection, with left leg fully engaged to avoid all possibility of the run-out left – and I could feel an answering twitch in that leg as I made the thought – and here I knew she would jump well, so I would ask her to fly. I did the same with my dressage test, but less often, and with less commitment.

Sports psychologists didn't invent mental rehearsal. Any boy who ever asked a girl out knows about it. Such techniques are natural in us: the psychologists merely formalised them. I heard of a 400-metres runner who was asked to go through a 50-second-long mental rehearsal of his race. He confessed moments later that it hadn't gone right: somehow he had imagined himself losing in the last strides. His psychologist told him to go through the whole exercise again. So he did – and threw up. Because it's physiologically impossible to run back-to-back 400 metres: the unique combination of aerobic and anaerobic demands on the human body are too great.

So at last I got to Day One, as well prepared as was possible. Favour and I put together a respectable dressage test. she was no great shakes at this and nor was I, but we were always pretty accurate, and that's half the battle. We then hacked back to Dragon Hall for a rest for Favour and a bit of serious fretting for me. I took off my jacket and tie and put on my cross-country colours: an old-fashioned school hockey shirt borrowed from a Lamma Island friend. It was yellow with black sleeves: Dragon Hall colours, by an excellent coincidence, so that would please Helen Wu. So long as I remembered to go through the start.

It was on the way back to Beas River that the terror really began to kick in. This is, after all, a sport in which you can break your neck. In the dreadful year of 1999, five professional riders died while riding in cross-country events, mostly in England, one of them a lovely lady I had rather a crush on. The ground is very hard, the obstacles are solid: they don't come apart when you clout one, as a show-jump does. A horse can refuse a jump, and that can happen at any time. Sometimes when this happens the horse stops dead and the rider carries on. At pace, on hard ground, and with hard obstacles, this is a straightforward way to pick up injuries. In jump racing a jockey is riding with very short stirrup leathers because he has very little need for lateral movement from his horse. Lateral movement is a serious concern for an event rider, and lateral movement comes from pressure of the rider's leg. So you ride long. When a horse falls under a jockey, the jockey is thrown clear. When a horse falls under an event rider, they sometimes come down together, one on top of the other, and not in the order they started off. And that's a killer.

I was, quite literally, taking part in the sport at the lowest possible level. With greater height and greater speed come greater dangers. But it's a fact that a fall from a bad horse hurts as much as a fall from a good one. There is an equality of danger here: perhaps an equality of terror. I know what it's like to risk my neck: I know what it's like waiting the wait before you take such a risk.

I was aware of all these things as I approached the start and warmed up, just at trot, while listening out for our names to be called. The problem of the flight-or-flight dilemma in sporting circumstances is that you know that, despite all the temptations, you're not actually going to run away. You know you're going to do it, even though a well-organised interior minority – but one with a very powerful lobby – is urging you to give up. It occurred to me, for example, that I could ride up to the starter and say: excuse me, I'm afraid I'm suffering from rather bad peritonitis, and so I'd better not ride in this event after all – because on thinking things through I realise that it *wouldn't be fair to the horse.*

All the time knowing I was going to do no such thing.

And then the go.

At once we rolled into a great big ground-eating canter, none of your bouncing vertical-power canters of the show ring: this was fast and purposeful and designed to get us somewhere. To the first jump: easy, inviting, a traditional soft start to get you and your horse in the mood, then off into the empty country looking for fences to jump. Preferably in the right order. And by about fence six I was in heaven. Every fence was a greater joy than the last.

There were the pleasures of speed and risk and my own daring, but there was also the curious, transcendent joy that is so hard to explain to the non-horsey. All explanations induce either disbelief or an inclination to vomit, or, of course, both. So apologies here.

But it's a shared thing, you see. It wasn't just me doing something. Sure, I felt the delight in sustained speed and movement that I knew in Chivalry Road during my lightning brief career as a great distance-runner, but this wasn't about the same fierce loneliness. There was the sense of cooperation, of being part of a team. I was flying, yes, but with borrowed wings, so I had a deep debt to the lender. It was about moving in synchronicity and in harmony with the beast beneath me. But it wasn't a sexual thing. Let's sort that out right away: horses and sex have a complex relationship, at least in the minds of people who have little to do with horses. It was a team thing: and you can't say, no, that doesn't work, because Favour was an unwilling conscript. Had she been unwilling she wouldn't have galloped, she wouldn't have leapt. She was responding to my eagerness, I to her delight in going along with me. Or was it the other way round?

There was one point when the course took us up a steep path to a lofty hilltop. We took a jump or two along the high, exposed ridge, following a track that snaked along the top with all China spread out below us. Then we hit the path that led down. A pretty damn steep path: walking up it, you'd have to use your hands in places. I had made a plan in my mental rehearsal: I was going to take a pull as we hit the top of the path and we would walk down in a sensible and sober fashion, taking up canter again as we reached the bottom and the last half-dozen fences before the finish.

It was at this point that the madness within me overflowed. A demon took over my body, my mind, my personality, my soul. And instead of taking a pull, I kicked on. After a surprised pause of perhaps a quarter of a second, Favour said: well, what the hell? Why not? In a great skittering canter she took the not-quite-vertical downslope with immense eagerness. I was at least smart enough to drop the reins and let her have her head so she was balanced and confident, and I stood in the irons and kept my own balance as we zigged and zagged down the path like a lone rider getting the message through in a Western. Thus at a new and still fiercer level of exultation we completed our descent. I had started up at the top as a novice rider: I hit the bottom as a horseman, not in terms of enhanced ability but in terms of commitment. It was a life-changing skedaddle. I had gone deeper into the terrors available on horseback and I had found joy.

We reached level ground and turned for home, taking the remaining fences with lickety-split confidence. We rode through the finish and I pulled her up, leaping from the saddle before she had fully halted. I loosened her girth before I gave her a brief but fulsome embrace, and once she had caught her breath – and I had – I led her back to Dragon Hall, noting that walking in riding boots is a sub-optimal experience.

I was inclined to think myself no end of a fellow as I made the long journey back to Lamma Island. That was in the rare moments when I could think at all. Mostly I was consumed by the intense nature of the experience: something that I could still feel echoing in my arms and legs, and perhaps most especially at my centre of gravity. Is that the most important chakra for a horseman? Riding is a matter of perfect stillness in the midst of furious movement. If you want to keep in balance with a galloping, leaping horse you need to move all the time: but you must synchronise your movements to those of the horse, so that it looks as if you are completely stationary. Your point of balance is over the horse's withers – shoulders – and it never moves relative to that point. But in order to keep it there you must move all the time to the rhythm of the horse. This was the intoxicating experience I had been through, and I had it then as I have it now: as yet another of those perfectly vivid psychokinetic memories.

And I was also inclined to think of myself as a pretty brave person: certainly not one associated with the wee sleekit cowrin' tim'rous beastie from the playing fields of Blagdons. But I've come to reconsider this verdict. Yes, sure, it's a bit brave: but it's not brave like plunging into an icy river to rescue a drowning child and it's not brave like standing up for your beliefs in hostile circumstances. I was brave in the way that I am generous when I hand out a quid to a beggar. I was doing something in order to savour my own good qualities, my own bravery, my own generosity. This savouring was not the whole point or even half the point of riding a horse across country: this wasn't bungee-jumping. But I really wasn't entitled to walk away from this and call myself a courageous man.

Sport is a courage-opp, as I said before, but it's not about courage of the 24-carat kind: the pure golden lovely thing that protects drowning children and truth. There is perhaps a cord that connects the winning shot on match point, the defiance of the bouncer barrage, the downhill skier and the cross-country rider with the genuinely great acts of courage that go beyond all superlatives, but it's a damn long one. Sport gives us a thousand opportunities every day to witness courage in action – grace under pressure – and it's a vivid experience because sporting courage reminds us – distantly but in inexpressibly vivid form – of the real thing. And what I did that day with Favour, and did many times subsequently with different horses, was not the real thing. It just felt like it: it just bloody well felt like it and as a result I felt ever so slightly like God almighty. So when I see a great athlete in a moment of triumph, I know. I understand.

I went back the following day for the showjumping phase of the competition. Favour was understandably weary and, as a result, our performance was a little flat, both in mood and in jumping ability. I had longed for the honour of finishing on our dressage score – that is to say, without any jumping penalties – but it was not to be. We had a couple down and finished third. And that, I am a trifle embarrassed to admit, was good enough for me.

Before I set off back to Lamma I sought out the timekeeper and asked how we had gone across country. The optimum time was 13 minutes: any slower and you get time penalties. Our time was eight minutes and 50 seconds. Bloody fool. The timekeeper didn't say that but he clearly thought it. And, had I nursed Favour around the course and completed in 12 minutes and 59 seconds, she would have had more oomph in her for the last day and we would have been far more likely to go clear. But I never thought of that. As I revealed my newly acquired talents as a horseman, so I also, without being aware of it, revealed my limitations as a sportsman. Not in terms of ability but in terms of attitude. It was clear that winning didn't interest me enough. Sport seemed to me far too good a thing to waste on winning. Certainly horses did.

## Chapter 20

# Enter the Dragons

We founded a football team because we wanted to improve society. It worked too, in a way. Our reward was a rather splendid adventure. It all took place on Lamma Island. It did so because tensions on the island had been rising for a year or so. When I moved out there I was the 17th *gwailo* – the Cantonese term for European – to take up residence: I was an exoticism, part of a tiny minority, and no threat to anyone. The Lamma residents got on with their jobs of fishing, market gardening, building three-storey houses in unlikely places and driving little tractors recklessly fast along the island's narrow concrete paths.

But the non-Chinese population started to grow and grow. The combination of (comparatively) low rent and exotic environment made it irresistible to many: travellers, bohos, chancers, lost souls, boozers, losers, artists with varying degrees of talent, writers, teachers of English as a foreign language, louche operators with undisclosed jobs and public school voices, druggers, gonzo journalists, musicians, dodgy dealers, carpenters, remittance men, a lapsed farmer, a nurse, strange grown-ups with stranger children, fantasists, liars, the sexually bizarre, criminals (at least three of whom went to prison) or any combination of the above.

And some of the Chinese residents began to resent this. Not the respectable ones, the suited commuters, the people with established businesses, the grown-ups. No: it was the corner boys with tattoos, the laddoes who smoked cigarettes and took to calling out Cantonese insults as we passed – some of which I understood – or who made silly remarks in high-pitched voices, mocking us to our faces. We were resented as outsiders, as people of apparently fabulous wealth (well, we could afford to rent a 700-square-foot flat or a room therein, and that was beyond the ambitions of many of our tormentors), inconceivable freedoms (no doubt about that) and quite extraordinary sexual licence (or so it must have seemed).

It was an American with religious connections called Lawrence who started it all off. He had read (being capable of reading Chinese) a poster inviting teams to a Lamma Island football tournament. He broke this news in the bar and suggested that we form a team ourselves. It would be good for community relations, he said. And he could play himself, he was OK, he told us. It was the pebble that started the avalanche.

Suddenly we were all footballers. Suddenly we were all OK. Well, not bad, as we English expressed such self-assessments. I seemed to be in a room full of former schoolboy internationals, all in their late 20s. Well, a good ten years later than 20, most of us, but we were all mad for the idea. End racial tensions and play football: I would save society and at least a thousand shots on goal. The combination was irresistible. So we arranged a trial: in theory as a test of ability, in practice to see if our enthusiasm survived the exit from the bar.

A bunch of us actually turned up. We wore odds and ends of gear, shorts, T-shirts, trainers. We didn't look like a bunch of crack athletes but, hell, we were there. And there was just one aspirant for the post of goalkeeper, so that was all right. It wasn't quite the first time I had played since those five-a-side days back at school. I had played in rambling pick-up games, sometimes of a half-decent standard, while I was at university, diving about and stopping the odd shot, and a few games of five-a-side while I was on local papers.

We gathered at one of the two local football pitches: not the Helipad Pitch but the Jungle Pitch. It was not a pitch for purists. It seemed to have been hacked from the jungle, for the vegetation on the island was rich and lush: a brief patch of bare earth, more or less level and carved from the side of a hill. There was a slightly drunken list from left to right if you were standing in the goal nearest the village. An overhit clearance or a too enthusiastic shot would end up deep in the bush, and often enough was never seen again. It was about the right size for matches between five or six.

I retain one sad – perhaps even tragic – image from that first trial. One of our number turned up in brand-new football kit, clearly bought for the purpose. This included equally brand-new football boots, not suitable footwear for a baked-earth pitch. His name, I think, was Jamie. He spoke in a gentle voice that reeked of rather embarrassed privilege. He had, it was believed, a good deal of money. He was not yet 30 and seemed to have come to Lamma to drink. Certainly no one had ever heard of him doing anything else: stuff like working, or eating. At this trial he was scarcely capable of speech. He could stand up, more or less, though the boots didn't help. He projected a sense of sweet bewilderment and sheepish resignation, inspiring all those around him to treat him gently in return. He moved on soon after that.

Asia is full of places for a white man to drink himself to death.

The rest of the trial went well enough. It seemed that several of our number had actually played before; one or two were comparatively skilled. John, a strapping fellow from the farmlands of Kent, involved in various business activities no one ever quite understood, showed a marked talent when the ball was in the air, while Pete, teacher and journalist, showed a driving delight in the fray that was to exemplify all we did. He acquired the nickname Red Pete, for his naturally high colouring was much exaggerated in action and passion, especially when the two were combined, as they usually were. As he glowed like a stop-light on a dark night over that first trial, it was clear that our team would never lack commitment.

And that was good. Sport is serious, no matter how little talent you possess. Sport exists in some kind of semi-civilised no-man's-land between laughter and combat: it is always trivial but never frivolous. Not, at any rate, in the minds of the players.

I did well enough at this kickabout to remain unchallenged as goalkeeper. I dived about and stopped a few, showed a decent level of physical commitment, and began to establish a working relationship with John the Farmer. He was powerful and confident, seizing control of the airways in front of goal. It seemed clear that my job was to lurk behind him and stop anything he let through. That, and take on the one-on-ones, when he was caught upfield. It was clear even from this practice that diving at feet would be a part of routine duties.

And we had a team. So we challenged the corner boys to a game, a warm-up before the tournament, and they took up the challenge with great enthusiasm. They were right to be enthusiastic: they played two or three times a week among themselves and we were fresh meat. It was a rambling, un-refereed match and they won it convincingly. They were much more skilful than us: they liked the ball down on the floor, they liked tricks, they liked passing. Their top man was very talented. I remember him beating me with a leaping scissor-kick from a ball played over his shoulder; he made contact with it a good three feet from the ground and I was never within commuting distance of the ball. 'All right, Pelé, good hit,' I said, applauding with admiration and a soupçon of bitterness. He laughed and lit a cigarette, it being half-time.

The tournament was the following Sunday. It was to last all day. We weren't ready, in the sense of being ready to beat anybody, but we had a team. And we needed a name: a name that the Chinese would relate to. Chinese, in all its forms, is a language based on monosyllables. Very many words sound a lot like very many other words: in Cantonese there are nine tones – notes of the scale on which you pitch your syllable – and the tone is often the only difference between two or more different meanings. These associations have a great deal to do with the mysteries of Chinese poetry as well as with the rhythms and superstitions of everyday life. Number four is unlucky because the word in Cantonese – *sei* – sounds very like the word for death.

There was a Lamma rural myth in which a *gwailo* had a missing dog. So he walked around the village knocking on doors, asking in Cantonese: 'Can you help me please? I cannot find my dog.' He was upset to be greeted by helpless laughter; it was only later that he learned he had been saying 'I cannot find my dick.' It follows, then, that Chinese love puns. A Lamma artist – and I know this one is true – had a series of business cards printed with his name transliterated into Chinese characters on the reverse side. A Chinese friend had done this for him: a friend who had yielded to temptation, alas. My friend's name was Shramenko; he was of Russian extraction, and so in many ways a typical Lamma resident. His name read in Chinese *Sam Mang Gow*. Fair enough. Except that it means three-dollar prick.

But we got the name for our football team pretty well right, I think. *Gwailo* means ghost people, a reference to traditional European pallor. It's often translated as foreign devil. So we were Gwai Loong. The Devil Dragons. Ready to come out on to the main football pitch of Lamma Island breathing fire.

# Chapter 21

# Emergency Exit

We chose to play in all white, for white is the Chinese funeral colour, perfect for the ghostly connotations of our name. Cindy, then my girlfriend and now my wife, inscribed each shirt with the Chinese characters for Gwai Loong. The competition took place in late May on a beltingly hot day, not at the Jungle Pitch but on the helicopter pad.

Soon after I moved out to Lamma, the Hong Kong government decided that Lamma was the perfect place for a power station. Our village, Yung Shue Wan, was divided on the subject, but it was generally felt that the government owed us something. So, after long consultation they decided that what we deserved was a slab of concrete. The area for the slab was reclaimed from the little harbour. It was a helicopter pad for emergency medical cases and a site for the annual opera festival (Cantonese opera, not *Rigoletto* and *La Bohème*). It's tertiary but in practice its principle use was as a football pitch. The Helipad Pitch. We were now a two-pitch town.

On a crowded and dramatically hilly island any open flat area is a rare and wondrous thing, so in some ways we were lucky to get it. But a concrete slab in a harbour has certain disadvantages as a football pitch. First, it's quite hard: have you ever tried diving across goal to tip one round the post on concrete? Or slide tackling? Or taking one of football's routine tumbles? Second, the ball is going to end up in the sea every now and again; eventually they put a fence round the slab, but it was never high enough. And third, concrete is a marvellous way of reflecting back the heat. A match on a sunny summer day really sucked the juices out of the players.

To this day I get cross when I hear an English or British sporting team of any kind complaining about the heat, saying that conditions are unfair, brutal, inappropriate, inhuman. We played on this concrete pitch – I know, I'm about to sound like *Monty Python*'s four Yorkshiremen – when the temperature in the shade – and of course there was no shade – was around 100 degrees Fahrenheit and the relative humidity around 100 per cent.

But that's one of the eternal truths of sport: if you have a taste for playing sport, you find a way. The urge to do so comes from deep in our natures. It's not part of the human condition: it goes much deeper than that. Play is part of our mammalian heritage: I've watched lion clubs at play; I've watched adult lions initiate play with cubs. So play happens and sport, above all else, is play. Lion play has its serious side: it's training for hunting, it's training for the fighting that will often be part of a lion's life. But it begins as play and is a kind of sport.

I've seen a thousand photographs of children playing sport in the most unpropitious circumstances: in refugee camps, war zones, slums, between railway tracks, under motorways, in remote rural areas, in deserts and in rainforests: pitches on a steep slope, with a tree in the middle, with busy traffic passing all around. Sport will out: it's part of what we do and who we are. A roasting concrete slab in weather that brings out a shirt-clinging sweat in a 50-yard walk: *look-shuurry*!

It was Tournament Sunday. We watched a couple of matches before it was our turn, and I was equally struck by the ball skills of the outfield players and the bizarre lack of commitment from the goalkeepers. In fact, for a few horrified minutes I wondered if there were special rules for this competition, in which goalkeepers weren't allowed to handle the ball. Then I wondered if goalies were forbidden to catch the ball and hold on to it. But no: it was just that no Lamma Island footballer wanted to keep goal. Perhaps it was a loss of face, the position for losers. So they punched where they should have caught, kicked where they should have gathered and didn't dive on to the concrete. Well, I was going to dive and see what the referee did about it. I was well padded. Cindy had improvised padding from foam packaging: a wodge of the stuff on each hip and loads of the stuff taped over knees and elbows. I looked not unlike the Michelin man and I aimed to give a three-star performance.

And then we were out there. In the roasting tray.

Perhaps the most shocking thing was the all-consuming nature of participation. The entire world shrank down to a little concrete slab. The problems of starvation, poverty, warfare, global crisis and the ecological holocaust had no meaning: nor did my professional and emotional concerns. All that filled my soul was the feet – always watch the feet – of the advancing opposition, the shapes their bodies made in action, the steep bounce of the ball on concrete, the positions of my colleagues, my own position in relation to that of John the Farmer. This is one of sport's great attractions. It's not just a negative thing, in the take-your-mind-off-your-troubles sense of the term: it's much better than that. When you play sport in the intense and confrontational manner of the territorial ball games, the entire world is comprehensible. That's because there is nothing in it except kick and run, shoot and pass, save and miss.

I have a theory about film. It goes like this. A film can be art, but that's not what film is best at. What film can do better than any other medium is to take you somewhere else – into a different world, one in which a man can step out into the rain alight with happiness and start singing while an orchestra strikes up to accompany him. Films can take you to another time, another place, another reality: to the Middle Earth of the hobbits, to a galaxy far far away, to the OK Corral, to a place where love always wins, to places where vampires lurk, to cities full of superheroes. And this is a fine thing to experience not just because it takes you away from reality – as the movies did during the Depression – but because entering a new world is an adventure in itself. Sport does that too. It does that for a spectator or supporter: and it does that a thousand times more vividly for a participant. Sport is an emergency exit from reality.

Observers often criticise professional athletes for their limited view of the world, for their lack of hinterland, for their inability to comprehend anything but the little world of action. But that's precisely what sport demands, at any rate while you're doing it. Sport is not asking you to become a person of infinite range and depth: rather, it demands complete commitment to a very small and very narrow thing. So don't criticise the footballer who only knows about football: that's the nature of the task. You can criticise the commentators, writers and pundits for their limited view of the world, because such people should see sport in the wider context of events, but not the people doing it.

What do they know of cricket who only cricket know? The question was asked by the great Trinidadian writer C. L. R. James. It's one worth asking: but the fact remains that a cricketer who only knows cricket can be damn good at his job.

I had a blinder in that game. Mostly expressed in one-on-ones with the opposing forwards. Our outfield players would be caught out up the pitch, and once again a lone forward would be through and I would rush from my line and dive at his feet. Any lack of commitment in the forward, any reluctance to take a fall on to the concrete, was at once exposed. Sometimes two of them would come through together, so I would charge the one and he would wait and pass and his colleague would put the ball into the empty goal. Sometimes I got to the passer before he released the ball. I stopped an awful lot of goals: but then I had an awful lot of opportunities. 'Well played,' they told me afterwards. 'It would have been seven*teen*-one without you.'

Yes, we lost 7–1, so I was aware of one of the truths of all team games: that you can lose but still feel happy about what you did. That's the great problem in being a manager or a partisan spectator: the only pleasure is victory. Defeat has no consolation. I was the hero of a disaster. Well, that was better than being the one who lost the game for the team. What do they know of victory who only victory know?

There were things for us all to savour in the defeat. First, we had actually played. We had done it. There was a satisfaction in just that: putting on a team shirt, trying hard and being found wanting. There was some consolation in the goal we scored as well: Little Ant, English teacher and baritone saxophonist, two or three inches over five feet, was the scorer. He received the ball about ten yards out with his back to goal, controlled it, spun and scored. He performed a pirouette through almost 270 degrees to do so, so putting the ball in the opposite side of the goal to the one expected, wrong-footing goalkeeper and defenders: a very decent goal that gave us a touch of respectability. Besides, as one of those Nostradaman coincidences would have it, we had been drawn against the best team on the island. Wouldn't do to have the *gwailos* winning.

We hadn't done OK. We were unfit, disorganised, and had forgotten, if we ever really knew, what it was like to play a football match. We lost, we shook hands all round and said well done, and then we had a beer. Who was free on Wednesday afternoon? We'd fix a match with Pelé's boys.

# Chapter 22

# Well Hard

It was probably the best pre-match team talk in the history of Gwai Loong FC. It was delivered by my brother-in-law Rob, Roob in the family. He was working for the British Council and he came to Hong Kong on business, staying, naturally, on Lamma. He was a footballer himself, a strapping, speedy and erratic right wing, so I found a place for him in the team that played on Sunday. And we had new and unfamiliar opponents that day.

'Right, lads,' Roob said. 'Let's give these Vietnamese refugees a hard time.'

We were playing a team of boat people. They had arrived in Hong Kong seeking sanctuary and they found a refugee camp. They were miserable, frustrated and bored, having been consigned to life's waiting-room. They were ethnic Chinese and Cantonese speakers. There had been trouble on Lamma a year or so earlier when a large number of refugees had been confined to the boat they arrived on, the *Skyluck*. This was moored off Lamma; in desperation the inmates cut the anchor chain and the boat drifted on to the rocks just off the island. The refugees got ashore only to be rounded up and confined to camps.

This, then, was a fine day out in a terrible time, and they made the most of it. I remember vividly my first touch of the ball in that match, which we played up on the Jungle Pitch. I went for a high ball – where the hell had John the Farmer got to? – against their centre-forward, a powerful lad, tall for a Chinese, about six foot. I caught the ball cleanly enough, and expected him to back off, as the Cantonese of the island usually did. Not a bit. He followed through with immense exuberance and we ended up in a pile on the ground. I remember his laughing face about an inch from my own. I think he offered me a hand up; even if he didn't, there was the cheery sense of challenge: a contest to be entered into.

As a generalisation, the Chinese players we came up against were not overkeen on physical confrontation. On the whole, they liked the idea of football as a non-contact sport: a showcase for clever ball skills. Gwai Loong embodied a more robust approach: one that won occasional grumbles, but which could be easily deflected by pointing out that this was a game rich in possibilities for physical contact. 'Men's game. OK?'

I was rather surprised by my ability – my willingness – to adapt to this. It seemed that the dark memories of Blagdons could be laid aside. It helped, of course, that our opponents were Chinese, and so I was seldom too heavily overmatched in terms of physique, and, it has to be said, in appetite for physical confrontation. More often than I would like, I had to defend a one-on-one, and I developed a technique: come off the line fast, dive *over* the ball, getting body between the opponent and the ball, the opponent and the goal. Lead with the shoulder, gathering the ball goalside of your own body. And if your shoulder takes the onrushing forward in the shins, you accept the bruises ... and if this contact should bring him crashing down on the baked earth of the Jungle Pitch or the bleached concrete of the harbour pitch, then, in the immortal words of Frank Bruno, that's cricket, Harry.

I collected a few whacks here and there, and dealt a few: nothing so very terrible. I got kicked in the shoulders and the back and once a hefty boot in the kidneys; a few forwards got skinned knees and shoulders from their tumbles, and sometimes this caused them to back off and sometimes it gave them a greater appetite for the struggle. Either approach had its points, so far as I was concerned. It was an extension of the lessons I had learned from competitive horseriding: sport is a more vivid experience when there is a certain amount of physical danger. When you need a small amount of courage just to take part. Not a lot: just enough to give spice. The possibility of getting hurt a little seemed to matter.

Please don't think I'm writing myself up here as some kind of hard-man enforcer: the idea is ludicrous. I note it here because it was a slightly odd experience. I had spent most of my life to this point thinking that I was the sort of person who shied away from physical confrontation, only to find myself going out of my way to seek it. I sought it in the form of sport rather than bar-room brawls: in a controlled environment, set about by rules and conventions, a context that permitted physical exuberance while at the same time keeping it within bounds.

You can find the same thing again and again in the semi-ritual sparring for dominance elsewhere in the animal kingdom. Giraffes can kill a lion with a single kick and could break each other's legs easily enough with a well-directed blow, but when they fight they go in for a sort of Indian wrestling with their necks. I've seen a cobra fight: they don't use their poisonous fangs, which might be a bit drastic, instead they coil around each other and test out each other's strength. Such dominance disputes are a serious form of play. Which is a fair definition of sport.

And in football, instead of punching and throttling and biting we settle on a convention of pushing and shoving with occasional shin kicks. And that works very happily for all concerned. Of course, for giraffes and for footballers, things can go wrong and serious injuries occasionally occur. But in the main, a safe and satisfactory way of giving and receiving bruises is an established part of many sports: and is one of its great attractions.

I can't remember too many details of the boat people match, save that it was pretty close and a damn good contest. I have an enduring memory of Roob playing on the wing in borrowed footwear. He had come to Hong Kong with nothing but business shoes. I lent him a pair of plastic-soled kung-fu slippers, which enabled him to run pretty fast, but not to stop or turn with any certainty. His occasional overshooting of the byline into the jungle enlivened an already lively occasion.

The fixture came about because one of the Gwai Loong players was teaching English in the refugee camp. We had a fine little rough-house of a game, and we treated our opponents to a few beers before they had to get on the ferry and return to camp, return to the waiting room. They had made the most of this brief foray into the world, I thought, as I savoured a certain tenderness around both shoulders and a Turneresque sunset made itself visible on my upper left arm.

# Chapter 23

# The Monsoon Match

It was Sunday afternoon on the Jungle Pitch in high summer. The cloud ceiling was a few feet higher than the crossbars on the goals. We were maybe 20 minutes into one of our regular matches against Pelé's boys when the rain started. And when it rains in summer in Hong Kong it rains. No half-measures. When I first came from England I thought: it can't rain like this for long, it'll slacken off in just a moment. But it doesn't. It rains like an English cloudburst for hours at a time. It's like the bit when Gene Kelly stands under the downpipe: instant saturation. There's no letting off when that state has been achieved: it carries on all day. On hard pavements the drops rebound knee-high. You get soaked under your umbrella from the atomised droplets.

So when the rain began to fall, our opponents as a man turned to flee. In England we play through the rain, so we gave them a terrible bollocking. Wimps! Come back and play football, you weedy buggers! What's the matter, can't take a drop of rain? The taunting had its effect. After a brief consultation, they decided they weren't going to back down to no *gwailos*, and if we wanted football in the rain then by God we'd get football in the rain.

It was perhaps the most glorious football match I ever played in. It was hard to see anything. Looking upwards at a high ball hurt your eyes from the hammer blows of rain. Faces, noses, bodies acted as streaming conduits for water. The ball's flight and behaviour was affected by the astonishing weight of water. Within half an hour or so three streams had established themselves across the pitch: not trickles but urgent fast-moving watercourses hurrying pell-mell down the slope, taking advantage of the undulations of the pitch. The outfielders had to leap or wade and occasionally tumble as they tried to keep an eye on both the ball and the streams. Naturally, the streams became a magnet for the ball, so the outfielders needed a new way of reading the game. When the ball joined the stream the smart player was already there to intercept it a few yards downstream.

It was wonderfully crazy for the goalkeepers, the ball exploding like a fragmentation grenade of water drops as it struck my palm. My protective foam padding turned into six bath sponges, each one trying to flop from its moorings. Before long the baked earth pitch had turned to mud. We were all filthy, but none so filthy as me. Accuracy was compromised: my throw-outs and kicks could go anywhere, but the problems of anyone controlling it, friend or foe, were close to insuperable.

They should play World Cup finals in conditions like these. That'd sort things out.

And on it went. On and on and on: for who could back down? Besides, the whole thing became intoxicating. It wasn't terribly cold, and we were all running about or at least diving about, and you can't get wetter than wet. There was an urchin delight in it: a bunch of grown men playing like kids in a junkyard and knowing no mother would rebuke us on our return home. We called a ceasefire when it began to get dark: with relief, it's true, but also with a little reluctance, a little sadness. We shook hands with a rather special warmth, exchanged pleasantries with affection. We had shared something a little out of the common run. Not everyone has played a three-hour football match in a monsoon; not everyone has played football on a pitch with three streams. Nor, I suppose, would we ever again.

I've no idea who won. Perhaps I hadn't even then. It was a high-scoring draw, no matter how many goals had been scored and how many conceded. It was another lesson in what is, perhaps surprisingly, the most ancient of sporting truths: that sport is not all, and perhaps not even mainly about winning and losing. Sport begins with the delight in doing it, and the delight in doing it with other people.

In a famous essay, the well-known goalkeeper Albert Camus – goalkeepers have a tendency towards existentialism – said: 'All that I know most surely of morality and the obligations of man I owe to sport.' He recalls his most fearsome opponent – who had the odd nickname of Watermelon – and decides that there was good even in him. They had shared something. And not just goals and saves and bruises.

The monsoon match had something of that. I felt a weird affection not just for my team but also for my opponents. And the two forms of affection were inextricable.

# Chapter 24

# Clever Trevor

We define ourselves by the choices we make. All the same, that's an idea we need to be careful with. It implies that by making these choices we decide what kind of person we're going to be. That's true only to a comparatively limited degree. It's not so much that these choices determine who we are: more than that they *reveal* who we are. Sport is a medium that dramatises this principle as vividly as it dramatises most things.

The significant decisions in our lives tend not to be the ones we reach after hours and days and sleepless nights of interior debate. Often they don't feel like decisions at all, more like the inexorable workings of fate. Sure, we are free, at least in theory, to make the opposite decision, to walk away, to do something completely different. But we don't. It's almost as if these decisions had been made already, and that we have no choice but to go along with them. Marriage is a little like that – well, it was with me. I didn't reach the decision to propose marriage by drawing up a credit and debit list: I just did it. So many big decisions are made not because of what you decide, but as a result of being the kind of person you happen to be.

You can see this in the simple dilemma of a batsman struggling against good bowling on a difficult wicket. Do you knuckle down, grind out the runs, value your wicket highly and somehow work yourself into a dominant position? Or do you take arms against a pitch of troubles, go for all-out attack and blast your way into form? Both approaches are valid; equally, both can fail. Both can excite admiration in success and derision in failure – and the choice of strategy tends to reveal the kind of cricketer you are. The decision is made long before you take guard: perhaps, to take an extreme view, at your birth, or even before it.

My farewell to Favour was just such a decision. It was important and significant and not made without reluctance, but, all the same, I was never going to go the other way. The truth was that after a season or two with Favour, a time in which I had learned to be a rider of reasonable competence, both in and out of competition, I had gone as far with her as I could. As far, that is, in terms of my education as a horseman. I had ridden myself out of the Novice Rider category: I could have chosen to ride her into Grade C. She was experienced and more than capable at this level. I could certainly have spent a season or two seeking glory with her, picked up a fair few ribbons – that's to say, rosettes, the things they give you if you finish in the top few – and cups and stuff. It's a process technically known as pot-hunting.

Nothing wrong with that either. It's all in the way these things take you. I could have had a great time pointing Favour at fences in the right order and kicking when it seemed appropriate, and I would have had the most wonderful fun. But I wouldn't have learned anything. I wouldn't have become a better horseman. And it seemed that this was what I wanted. I turned down fun: I rejected victory. Sport has more to offer than either: more to offer than both put together.

I took on a new horse. He was 11 years old and had spent the last eight of them as a racehorse in Hong Kong. He was a stocky, tough little Aussie thoroughbred, a dark bay with a big white face and, as we liked to say at Dragon Hall, he had two paces, walk and piss off. Not entirely true: he had a choppy little trot and a splayed-out canter that was always trying to be a gallop. It was my task to turn him into a showjumper and an eventer. His name was to be a great source of embarrassment when it was announced over the PA: Fairy Fun. I called him Trev, short for Clever Trevor, from the Ian Dury song. This was not an ethereal horse.

It was an enthralling business. It took time, but when you have a progressive horse the entire world is a good place. I remember speaking to Charlie Whittingham, the great American racehorse trainer, and I asked why, in his mid-80s, he hadn't retired. He said, in a fabulously deep growly voice: 'Simon, I got a young horse.' Meaning that he had several hundred. 'No one with a young horse ever committed suicide.'

Trev was hardly young, but he was starting a new life and he took to it with great enthusiasm. Once I'd got the feel of him I took him out hacking around the paths and hills and jungles of Beas River. Imagine the joy of it. Here was a horse that had spent his life in a multi-storey stable block in the middle of the city, and whose only time without a roof over his head came in morning exercise, setting out before dawn to walk through the streets of Happy Valley with muffled hooves and then cantering or galloping on a sand track with the other horses. Now he was out on his own in a wild sort of place, walking at his ease, snacking from the branches, out in the big real world, often just lazing along with his head swinging free, his rider holding on to the buckle of the reins. Partly this was done for the pleasure of it, but the pleasure was also part of an education. Trev was relearning life's possibilities, clearing his head of the claustrophobia and limited aims of his existence and enjoying – quite literally – wider horizons. He was able to relax, take exercise and become a new-made thing.

Back at Dragon Hall I worked with some commitment at the formal part of his education. I had plenty of advice and help; I had neither the experience nor the ability to do it alone. Gradually I established a better trot and, better still, a controlled canter. He got the hang of the technical demands of his new life, which involved working in circles rather than straight lines. He learned to work with the appropriate bend in his body. He learned to 'listen to the leg', as horsey people say: sensing pressure from the rider's lower leg and moving away from it as we performed endless 20-metre circles.

It was utterly absorbing. At the beginning I didn't know when Trev would revert to racehorse type and piss off, as was his birthright, and I didn't know when he might take exception to his education, as I overtaxed him, throw a hissy fit and buck a bit. He always had a fair buck on him.

He only got me off once in the training arena, very early in our relationship, when the third or fourth buck was too much for me. I landed flat on my back on the sand, all the breath knocked out of me. I remember lying there thinking, with huge reluctance: bugger. Now I've got to be bloody brave. I have, in the most literal terms, got to get back on the horse. I didn't want to, but I very badly wanted to keep on riding. So I found a bit of air from somewhere and started breathing it. I swung myself back into the saddle. Gave him a bit of a pat. And slowly worked up to a point when I could repeat the exercise. This time it seemed to go all right.

I had a progressive horse. I had a beer afterwards – I always did – but it was unnecessary. I was already intoxicated.

# Chapter 25

# Promotion

I became the dawn rider. My day was over before anyone else's had begun. The Novice Horse events generally began at eight, to get them out of the way before the more sexy stuff started ... though this was actually a pretty entertaining class, novice horses being infinitely capable of making fools of experienced riders. So I would sleep on the sofa of a friend who lived in the New Territories, catch the first train heading north from Sha Tin and get to the showground with Trev a little after seven. No Liz to nursemaid me these days, and no need for her: I knew what I was up to. And almost as soon as I started riding Trev in competition, we started to pick up ribbons. The training had gone well: patience and repetition had done their work, along with plenty of good teaching. I knew I was capable of doing the task ahead of me. The question was, how well?

I was still nervous. Show days did weird things to my metabolism. I couldn't eat at all, not a thing, though I sometimes managed one of the unbelievably disgusting egg sandwiches on the ferry home, and you have to be in an extraordinary state to get one of those down. But I was no longer nervous in a trembly oh-my-God sort of way. I was nervous as in keyed up. Wholly tuned in to the task. So much so that the natural needs of the body were put on hold. My warm-up was calm and to the point: half an hour of good flatwork, looking as ever for suppleness and cooperation. A single practice fence. And then into the ring. And here I would be concentrated and purposeful. Nothing else existed. I was able to find some relaxation: I didn't ride tense. I constantly reminded myself to breathe deep, and as I rolled into a short-striding canter I would tell myself to drop my shoulders and sink into the saddle. Don't just sit there: ride. At my best I was sympathetic, forgiving when I needed to be and decisive when circumstances called for it.

Minimum requirements you will say, and you'll be right. The point is that I had acquired them. I was no prodigy, but I could ride an ex-racehorse – one who

12 months earlier had been plying that trade – over a course of jumps and, what's more, ride him clear. Not that I got cocky about it: horses – particularly thoroughbreds – have a tendency to stop people getting above themselves. The next humiliation is never so terribly far away, and I had my share of those, though mostly in private. Over the course of our season in Novice Horse we both got the hang of what we were doing. And because I had done all the training myself, there was a special kind of satisfaction in this. I couldn't have found that pot-hunting with Favour.

I remember the first time we picked up a ribbon, a minor placing that followed a confident clear round and an undemanding clear round in the jump-off. I didn't cut corners and gallop: I wanted to give the horse confidence rather than fluster him. Afterwards, delighted to my soul at this shiny satin endorsement of my horse and my horsemanship, I was daft enough to say: 'And I'm pleased for the horse.'

I meant it with complete sincerity. As if Trev would be back in his stable thinking happily about his own achievements, feeling better about himself. And perhaps thinking: we did well today, me and my rider, and I'm pleased for *him*. Absurd. All the same, there is something more to this than the usual anthropomorphic horsey bullshit that alienates so many people.

What I meant was that it wasn't just about me. Or, rather, that it didn't feel like that. There was a sense of the team thing involved: the sense of being on a shared journey, a joint adventure. I don't know how illusory that was. I can't speak for Trev. But certainly, so far as I was concerned, there was a growing sense of loyalty and trust. I knew that I could ride at a certain kind of fence, and that if I got the approach right he would do his best to jump it. Which meant I could commit to the jump by throwing my weight forward, which in turn made it easier for him to jump. A classic example of a sporting virtuous circle, in fact. The fact that you're doing it well means that you can do it better.

Thus sport became a matter of sober routine. Do it seriously. Do it with complete sincerity. And find a deeper satisfaction than thrill-seeking, having a go, giving it a lash. I didn't ride in a yee-ha, bonnets over the windmill style, the style with which I had ridden Favour around the cross-country course. I had moved on, and by doing so I had a distant glimpse of what it must be like doing sport for a living. Progress could be measured. If I won a certain number of ribbons Trev and I would be promoted to Grade C: bigger fences and more demanding courses. I was eager to do that. First there was the satisfaction of promotion, a touch of putting people right. Yes, you thought I was a bit of a cowboy, a bit of tear-arse show-off, but now you have to admit that I'm a horseman. A serious competitive horseman. I didn't get on a made horse and just point and kick. I don't just do steering jobs. I got on a horse that had never jumped in his life and just look at us now: we're beating some of the top riders in Hong Kong because my novice horse is better than theirs and he's better because I've put in the hours.

I often came up against the man who ran the Jockey Club riding school in Pok Fu Lam, on Hong Kong island. He would generally bring a couple of horses from his stable and whirl them round the Novice Horse competition. He was a damn good rider – much better than me – and he rode to win. Every time. No question of long-term planning and giving the horse experience: he just went for it. When he went clear he beat me every time, for he would ride the jump-off flat out: make the horse turn, make the horse jump fences at a 45-degree angle. When he hit a fence I would generally beat him, because I tended to have a double-clear. But I never won a red ribbon. Never got a first place. He got several.

I should have got at least one. It was our last competition in Novice Horse. We were at the top of our game, and the opposition was clearly beatable. This was our day. Just before we went in, Sally, who by then was running Dragon Hall, gave me an urgent instruction: 'Don't go clear! If you can't help it, ride a technical!' She wanted me to ride a circle in the middle of the show ring, to cross our tracks, which counts as technical refusal and three faults. She wanted Trev to stay in Novice Horse; she had decided he wasn't ready for Grade C. I was furious at this and didn't know whether or not to obey. I think if I'd done what Sally ordered I would have been the subject of official censure, but it never happened. With my mind all muddled I managed to present Trev at a fence all wrong, and, rare thing for him, he knocked it. Thump. Four faults. And after the show, we were promoted anyway, on the committee's discretion. Good call: I didn't want to spend next season pot-hunting in Novice Horse. I wanted to try the big stuff.

I can't blame Sally too much for this, even though she got it wrong on several levels. The fact is, as I knew from the moment that we hit the fence, that this was my responsibility. My responsibility to ride into the fence properly, my responsibility to clear my mind of doubt.

Mind. It was a taste of how much that sort of thing matters. It all seemed so simple on Streatham Common: John Murtagh scored more goals and hit more fours than I did because he was better. Now here was me and Trev, the best combination in the competition, losing – getting nothing whatsoever – because the rider's mind was all mixed up. The great simplifications of sport can only be experienced when your mind is right. Sport invites a right mind, with its marvellous combination of simplicity and self-importance, but you have to meet it halfway. And here I had failed.

But hell and damnation, we were in Grade C.

# Chapter 26

# Notes from Everest

Two things happened as a result of Gwai Loong's entry into the sporting life of Lamma Island. The first was the easing of some of the social tensions, the second was that we got quite good. I'm not sure if these were surprising developments, or simply inevitable.

I can't speak for every non-Chinese person on the island, but certainly the vibes in the main street of Yung Shue Wan were infinitely more agreeable so far as I was concerned. I was no longer invited to have sex with my grandmother when I passed the corner boys. These days the banter was infinitely more sophisticated. 'Next time Chinese win, OK?'

'No chance. Next time we win, OK?'

And on and on: eternal banter, part of the birthright of humankind. Well, of boykind anyway. Sport had given us a language in common, a vehicle for expressing a complex mixture of rivalry and not-quite friendship. Sport allowed us to deal with each other as fellow-humans rather than as members of different races. It's one of the great truths of humanity: if he plays football he must be all right.

George Orwell was wrong. In his famous essay on sport, in which he wrote about a British tour of Moscow Dynamo, he stated that 'if such a visit had any effect at all on Anglo-Soviet relations it could only be to make them slightly worse'. The emergence of Gwai Loong FC actually made Anglo-Chinese relations on Lamma Island slightly better. Quite a lot better so far as I was concerned. 'Hey, Sai-meun!' That being a Chinese version of my name, which translates, I was delighted to learn, as 'Western Literature'. 'Sai-meun! Tomorrow we score many goals!'

'No way. I'll stop 'em all.'

Football is mock war but, as said before, it can only take place in times of peace. War minus the shooting, Orwell said, but shooting is quite a big thing to take out of a war. In fact, war without shooting is quite a lot like peace. Even though there were occasional outbreaks of temperament on the field. One of these was the affair of

Mark Wong's penalty. It was a bit of a flashpoint because Mark was the best player on the island, and even in pick-up games he only played with other very decent players. This was a damn good team, then.

And we were beating them. By then we were all a lot fitter, which meant defence and attack were no longer an either/or. We got organised and man-marked, which the Chinese teams hated. More importantly, we developed an understanding of the rhythm of football matches. We knew what we were about. John the Farmer and I knew how to work together; we both knew pretty well what the other would do next. We did far better than the Ancient Mariner, who stoppeth one of three.

So against Mark Wong's boys we were leading by the odd goal with the match more or less at an end. It was a major shift in the balance of footballing power and we felt pretty damn good about it.

Except that they had a late attack and a shot hit Pete on the hand.

'Ha'-ba'!'

It wasn't handball. It was clearly ball to hand. But these un-refereed matches must be played to a consensus and our opponents were adamant. To be fair, they tended to play that way among themselves: if the ball hit the hand it was handball, no nonsense about intention and interpretation. We took another view. Hard words were spoken. Pete, always passionate, was in the forefront. 'Pelé, you're a fucking cheat!' Immortal words.

It was, then, a moment of high drama when Mark placed the ball on the ground – no luxury like a spot to place it on, this was the Jungle Pitch – and backed up, looking at me and my goal to weigh up his options.

I had developed a theory about penalties. You make a simple calculation based on two pieces of information. You know from observation if the player is right- or left-footed. And you know from the way he plays whether he is straightforward, or whether he fancies himself as a bit clever. The natural swing is across the body, so the fancy swing away from the body and aim for the opposite corner. So the formula I had worked out goes like this: right-foot straightforward and left-foot fancy-dan, dive right; left-foot straightforward and right-foot fancy-dan, dive left. Mark was very skilful but in this moment of drama I fancied him to play it safe and go straightforward.

So I went into my stance. Arms up, trying to fill the goal, trying to make the target look small. And in his backswing I committed. A touch early but what referee would call me back? Right, dive right: try and reach as far as the damn post.

Not a great penalty. That, as it happened, was nearly my undoing. The ball was hit halfway between the middle of the goal and the right post and I had to reach back on myself to find it. I managed to get a forearm and a bit of thigh in the way: I stopped it and there was John between Mark and the goal, shepherding the ball back to me. No back-pass nonsense in those days.

So the match ended. I shook hands with Mark and Pelé and the rest and went for a beer. I felt I deserved it.

So, yes indeed, I have known glory. Sport is not only a courage-opp: it's also a glory-opp. It's not just the great champions who experience glory. When I see them lifting the cup, kissing the medal, weeping on television, thanking their parents, talking about God, trying to be cool, trying to remember to say nice things about the opponent, explaining that it hasn't sunk in yet, I know how they feel. As someone who has dived off the side of the pool knows how the great Fu Mingxia felt when she dived from the 10-metres platform with the cityscape of Barcelona spread out beneath her, as someone who has drunk half a lager knows that it's like to sip the nectar of the gods, as someone who has climbed a hill knows what it is like to stand with Hillary and Tenzing on the summit of Everest, so I, who saved Mark Wong's penalty to ensure that Gwai Loong were, at least for an afternoon, the best football team on Lamma Island, know what it's like to win the World Cup.

# Chapter 27

# Zen in the Art of Goalkeeping

It was time for another major tournament on Lamma Island but this time Gwai Loong were contenders. That was glory enough to be going on with, but naturally we wanted a bit more. Little Ant was off travelling somewhere, so we were short of a forward, and it was here that I anticipated the twenty-first century tactics of the game by inventing both the false nine and the high press. I suggested, and John and Pete, as manager and captain, went along with it, that the answer to the missing striker problem was to play without one. Instead we would draft in Chris the Carpenter, who had little skill but was immensely fit. His job was not to try and score goals or even to kick the ball all that much. But every time the opposition defenders had the ball, he was to harass them, run from one to the other as they passed, until they were fed up with him and fed up with the ball.

It was a beltingly hot day. The opposition were pretty good. Things were fairly equal, but Pete, aflame with the intensity of the big occasion – and it was a big occasion, believe me – broke away and scored. After that, the opposition camped down in our half and we were extremely busy. Then crisis. We conceded a free-kick just outside the penalty area, and hastily formed a wall to cover the right-hand side of the goal, while I covered the rest of it. Good plan, except the ball went straight through the wall at ankle height. Not ideal. But there I was wrapped round the ball in what was almost a foetal position, holding on to it for once – handling was never a strong part of my game – as the opposition forwards charged in at the goal. Pete's hand on my shoulder. 'Good as a goal, that.'

You remember these things.

Even if his words came from a desire to inspire rather than simple awe at my achievement. Pete scored again and we won 4–1. I have no recollection at all of the goal we – I – conceded. Funny that. And even Chris scored. He received the ball about a yard in front of goal and attempted to chest it down and volley home. He scored direct from his belly. Not a goal to be lightly forgotten, then.

There is a simple joy in winning. In winning as part of a team. You feel protected from all the bad things that could ever happen. It's not quite a master of the universe thing, and that's because of the sharey part of it all. I couldn't have felt this good if Pete and the rest hadn't scored their goals; they couldn't have felt this good if I hadn't saved that free-kick; none of us could have felt like that if John the Farmer hadn't protected the goal as if it was the Aberdeen Angus bull he had once worked with. The sense of being a little bit fabulous was mixed with gratitude: gratitude to the people who played alongside me, and a more abstract gratitude that I could be numbered among such company. I reckoned we'd get to the final. I reckoned we might win the whole damn tournament.

We, eh? Fine word.

But I missed the next round and we lost. I missed it because I had a chance to go to Japan and I took it without a second's thought. Another of those self-revealing decisions. I left not without a pang, but certainly without hesitation. The match turned on a clash of heads, a goal scored when one of us was down on the floor covered in blood. The referee waved play on and they scored.

Perhaps if I'd been there I'd have stopped them. Perhaps I wouldn't. How would I know? I wasn't there.

But there really was no choice. Tokyo was pretty wonderful and the spell of the Zen gardens of Kyoto has been on me all my life. I reread Basho and found a life companion. The trip gave me material for a couple of bits of journalism, and that was the way I earned my living; I placed a piece with the best paying travel magazine in Hong Kong. I have no regrets at all about going, but a profound regret at my poor skills in the art of bilocation. I wish it hadn't come down to a choice. But it did and I made it.

In doing so I understood that the difference between amateur and professional is not in getting paid. It's the extent to which that activity controls your life. Sport was not invented so that it might become the principal motivation and structure of a person's life. Sport was imagined as a complex and ambivalent pleasure that should coexist with all the other parts of life, some equally frivolous, some far less so.

By seeking Basho in the middle of a football tournament I was asserting the right of the old amateur. Amateur means lover, from the Latin, and I had the right to love sport among a great number of other things.

That doesn't make me superior to any professional athlete. It's the fact that sport matters so immensely to its leading participants that makes spectator sport such a riveting spectacle across the world. The fact that it matters so much is what inspires the greatest of athletes to their greatest performances.

I chose Ryoanji. It's all in the way these things take you.

# Chapter 28

# Dodgy Keeper

That joy in victory, that head-spinning sense of We, being part of Us against Them – that's all well and good but it's paid for in hard currency. And not just in the routine disappointment of defeat. The deeper pain comes when you are the cause of defeat. If that doesn't give you pain, victory will bring very little pleasure.

The problem with a concrete football pitch – in a way worse than falling on it – is the bounce. A ball dropping from a height can rise again with devastating steepness. If it does so a foot or so outside your penalty area, the goalkeeper has a dilemma: hang back and try and grab it as it comes down again? Or try and gather it as it rises, while trying to stay within the goal area?

Twice in half an hour I made the wrong choice. Went to meet the ball and miscalculated the bounce. Twice in half an hour the ball went over my head – a terrifyingly improbable distance over my head – rising as if powered by a sudden blast from a jet engine, or as if yanked skywards by a mischievous cherub who had the ball on a long string. Each time the ball carried on, as if operated by a homing device, into the goal. Once can be regarded as a misfortune, yes, I know.

I was quite unable to join my dear team-mates at half-time. Instead I sat with my back to one of the posts for a bit of a think. Knowing that it looked as if I was dramatising my remorse, as if I was begging for sympathy. But in truth that was the last thing I wanted. I couldn't face their disappointment and, worse than that, I couldn't face their decency. Bad luck, Si, brute of a bounce, never mind, mate, you won't do that again anyway. No. Let me have my bit of a think and then I'll try and get it right next time. But try to do so without being a hero and doing something even more stupid.

A goalkeeper puts himself in that position to a greater extent than an outfield player. In a sense it's why we do it: to know that those people running about so madly are depending on you. It's great when you get it right for them: it follows that getting it wrong is a reasonably ghastly experience.

For me there was an added layer of pain in my failure. It was as if my bluff had been called: as if my pretensions to be a sportsman were laid bare. I felt on that unpleasant afternoon that I had revealed myself for what I really was: not the dashing diving saviour of Gwai Loong but the skiving wimp of Blagdons.

For a professional athlete – one who is, by his ability and his choices, unable and unwilling to take the Japanese option – such things are infinitely worse. When I got it wrong, it was as if a part of me had failed. When a real footballer gets it wrong, it's as if his whole being is invalidated, his whole life is in vain. That's why big-time sport is such a tough calling: because failure is total. 'It's not nice going into the supermarket and the woman at the till is thinking, "dodgy keeper",' said David James, former England goalkeeper. And it's true that such failure is more obvious for a goalie.

When you fail in top-level sport you fail completely and in public. Think of the worst cock-up you ever made in your professional life, and then imagine it being witnessed by, say five million people. Or ten. Or a billion. That's what it means to fail in sport. We see thousands of images from sport in which people raise cups, kiss medals, punch the air, knee-slide, raise their arms, leap into the air. But the only reason that these wonderful things can happen is because there is someone a few feet away with his head in his hands. Or his back against the goalpost.

Sport is cruel, but I knew that by then. I also knew that if you have never savoured sport's cruelties you have never played it properly. If it doesn't hurt – at some relatively deep level – you're not doing it right.

# Chapter 29

# Three Times a Champion

Grade C was an adventure. But a good one. Demanding for us both, but right from the start Trev and I were able to get round without elimination and eventually we managed to get clear rounds. Even the odd ribbon. And I have one very clear memory of that time: one of those psychokinetic sequences that stay vivid for years.

The great step up to Grade C was not just the increased height of the jumps – intimidating to both me and Trev, laughable to someone who has just watched the Olympic Games – but also the challenging nature of the course. Especially the treble. Three fences in a row: physically demanding for any horse, and mentally very taxing indeed for a horse who spent eight years of life on the racetrack specialising in the 1,000-metre sprint.

There's a lot to go wrong in a treble. The approach is scary: it looks to the horse as if you're asking him to jump one massive fence about ten feet high: a great wall of poles. Even if this prospect doesn't stop him altogether – and be sure that in practice it often did just that – he tended to approach the first fence very warily, which meant that he had no bounce and impulsion to take the second and third. There's an awful thing that can happen with a treble: hit the first and you hit the other two as well. You establish a rhythm of failure. If a horse loses straightness and rhythm, he loses balance and so he will make error after error. No time to put it right in the middle of a treble.

It's an enthralling thing to take on. It requires a troubling bit of self-examination. When an error happens, how do you apportion blame? Did you get it wrong, must try harder? Or did he make an error, which you must work on in practice? Humility is a good start, but it's never the whole answer. That's a useful truth for anyone trying to do sport – or anything else – a shade better than before. I was always too self-critical, doubtless from all those lessons I had got from fierce female instructors telling me how useless I was.

Now here's a tip for all aspiring riders: never try to learn from watching a champion. I once spent a morning with the great Mark Todd, double Olympic gold medal-winner. And I had no idea what he was doing. The horses just jumped. He just sat there. Or so it seemed. The corrections were invisible to the naked eye at full speed.

So there I was with Trev, riding into a treble. I can remember the details: it was at Beas River, the fences slightly downhill, so you don't want to rush or you'll get too close to the first fence and knock it on the way up. There was nothing else in the world except me, my horse, and three fences stretching ahead, towering above. I felt Trev's slight hesitation as we turned towards the treble, so I counter-suggested with my legs and he opened his stride a little and took the first fence competently. As he landed he thought for a second about running out left, but I read the thought even as it came to him and corrected with a soft touch of the right rein, a hint of pressure from my left leg. He took the second well but thought for a second about carrying on in the direction of my correction and running out right. So I put in a touch of left rein, hint of pressure from right leg. All this while leaping forward in the saddle three times, diving at the horse's head, moving my hands so that the pressure on the reins remained constant and didn't affect the bit in his mouth, neither poking far forward and giving him the option to change direction, nor – infinitely worse – holding him back. If you watch people learning to jump you will see horses sailing over fences with the rider leaning back and holding on by means of the horse's mouth: and, yes, I did that too, poor old Favour.

But not now. We were over and clear, and any non-horsey spectator would have thought that the horse just carried me over and I was only a passenger.

And that's how it should look.

The thing is, my corrections were to a large extent pre-emptive. If you like, I had perceived the intention to sin before the sin could be committed, and that is at the heart of good riding. That way you don't need to make large and dramatic movements: a small nudge, a tiny tweak – part of the constant dialogue of riding – and the horse continues on the straight line or the curve you have asked for. Jump jump jump: and not a pole disturbed. Is that not glorious? It was for me.

That sense of physical and mental mastery – however tenuous, however brief – is one of the more complex pleasures in sport. It's what you strive for perhaps more than anything else. It's a pleasure that comes from playing sport at any level, with any degree of competence: that almost out-of-body sense of being in command of your mind, yourself, your environment. Sport gives you an opportunity to savour, however fleetingly, that master-of-the-universe thing. And no matter how tiny that universe is, it's still a moment that can live with you forever. So much so that the physical memory of jumping that treble has persisted for more than 30 years. I can still feel those corrections: right hand and left leg, left hand and right leg. And Trev's vast self responding minutely but utterly appropriately.

I don't care how pathetic that may seem to you or, for that matter, how pathetic it genuinely is. I was there, I did it, I felt great; and even as I recall it, I still feel great. I never took any such moment for granted – they were too rare, and I had spent too long failing. So perhaps they are more wonderful for me than for the great ones of sport. Which means that I can consider myself luckier than the greatest. Certainly I was champion of that treble moment and it was wonder enough to be going on with.

We may or may not have got a ribbon at that show. I can't remember, so obviously it wasn't as important as jumping the treble clear. I just revelled in the combination of acquired technical ability, training (horse and rider both) and physical commitment. A showjumper must be both bold and nit-pickingly pedantic. This wasn't sport as in victory, as in winning prizes: this was sport as a measure of personal achievement, laced with the physical exhilaration of doing it right at speed, and at some feet (not all that many, I know) above the ground. This wasn't quite the same as the experience of competing with intensity and winning and losing becoming irrelevant. This was a very vivid sense of achievement. The satisfaction came not just from taking part in a meaningful competition: it came from the certainty that Trev and I had performed just about as well as Trev and I were capable of performing. I didn't need a ribbon or a cup to tell me about it, even though that would have been nice. It was confirmation of the old truth: there are satisfactions in sport to be found well away from victory.

# Chapter 30

# All in the Golden Afternoon

There was one last golden afternoon for me and Gwai Loong FC. It came one burning July Sunday on the concrete pitch by the harbour. By this time it was the custom for teams to gather there at the weekend. There tended to be around half a dozen of these, and a way of operating established itself. The first two teams to turn up played against each other. When you conceded a goal, you left the pitch and the third team to arrive took over. Concede a goal and you're off, back at the back of the queue, not playing again until your turn comes around. This could be a little frustrating on a leaky defence day – wait an hour and play five minutes – but sometimes you got on a run and had a merry time of it. That Sunday we got into the mother of all runs.

We were out there first, and played ourselves in while we waited for our first opponents to turn up. We were pretty strong that day: Little Ant was back and, for what it's worth, so was I. We took on the first team to arrive, and soon scored a goal to send them back into the shade. Then we did the same with the next, and the next … and as we did so a kind of magic took hold of all of us. We couldn't go wrong. Passes were finding colleagues, tackles were halting opponents, shots were finding the goal. It seemed not only that the world had suspended its troubles but that time itself had ceased to pass. We were locked in a bubble of perfection. At the back, John the Farmer commanded the air while I stopped everything that got past him. Pete, glowing like a flame, was playing attack, midfield and defence all at the same time, while still finding opportunity to shout urgent instructions at everyone else.

It was a collective magic. It wasn't that one or two of us were on form: it was as if good form – the best form – was a virulent infection that had spread through the team like a reverse plague, bringing life and joy and fulfilment. There is always a pleasure in sharing victories and defeats, but this was on another level entirely. We were taken, together, beyond our usual capacities, and each person's good work brought the best from the rest.

On and on the afternoon continued. The waiting teams waited, came on in their turn, fresh and full of ambition and found they could do nothing. Sometimes, as we grew weary, we would have to defend in depth, but that was not dismaying. Not at all. We were into the rhythm of it now, playing with complete certainty. And then the clearance, the breakaway, and often as not, the goal. One blazing hour carried on into the next. Ant took a breather behind the goal – occasional substitutions were permitted – and was dripping as if he was taking a shower. 'I've got to stop,' he said. 'But I can't. I keep scoring goals.' And then he was back on the concrete and scoring another. We were all – more or less literally – on fire.

Word went round the island: the *gwailos* have taken over, someone's got to get them off. By this time we had been playing for more than two hours. We were stoned blind on exhaustion and, above all, by the spell of magic: by the fact that we were playing together (and perhaps individually) as we had never played before and would never play again. It was this awareness that kept us out there playing as the sun cooled ever so slightly above us.

As a result of the emergency instructions spreading out from the football pitch, some of the best players on

Lamma appeared as if by magic before us. We held them off and then broke: Ant scored again thanks to a burst of scurrying pace that seemed impossible so late in the day. Another of the crack teams came out. This really was a good bunch, often too grand for these Sunday afternoon free-for-alls. Mark Wong was, of course, among them: they would surely finish us. I could hardly stand in goal. Lord knows what the rest felt.

It was then that we made our first real mistake of the afternoon. John went up for a corner and they cleared it, and there was only me against two of them on a fast break; by then no one, not even Pete, was capable of chasing back the length of the pitch. I faced the man with the ball; when he reached the edge of the area he chipped a fine cross. As I adjusted my position I saw the second player measure his header calmly, almost smiling as he did so. He knew he had got it right. He knew he had got me.

The ball looped back again, this time over my head. I was stranded, outnumbered, outdone. We had been breached at last. Our reign was over. The ball was past me. I was beaten. We were beaten.

No we bloody well weren't.

No, we weren't, because, as if it were a performance we had long rehearsed together, I was already leaping up and diving. Diving *backwards*, as if making the preliminary movement for a back-flip. I dived below the curving flight of the ball and reached back, my right hand more or less underneath the crossbar – and I found the ball. I had enough heft to deflect it upwards and it cleared the crossbar. Corner. And I was receiving disbelieving buffets of joy from my team-mates, who had by this time made the long journey back from the other end of the pitch. The corner came: John headed clear, Pete took it upfield, Little Ant scored.

So we called it a day. Three hours of football was enough. Three hours of perfection: more than any one has a right to. We shook hands all round with all our opponents who were still around and then crawled to the bar, stinking and sodden as we were. Some things need a little acknowledgement.

You watch a football team – any football team – and wonder why they're so good one day and so bad the next. Or you see a team playing like second-raters suddenly turn into world-beaters after conceding a goal. You wonder what's come over them: but, then, so do they. You can put it down to a manager's team talk, or a captain's example, or the will of the crowd – but in truth nobody understands, nobody knows, nobody can predict when it will strike, and when it's struck, nobody knows when it will wear off. It's a capricious gift that comes in all team games, but in free-flowing football more than any other. I felt as if I had received a gift from the great god of teams: but I also know I played my part in the process that made it happen. I know it wasn't magic, in the Harry Potter sense of the term. I also know that it felt exactly like magic. I never knew it again but to have felt it once was something.

# Chapter 31

# The Gate Closes

It wasn't quite the last time I rode Trev in competition, but there was something final about what took place. It happened at Lo Wu. They had acquired two striking new fences: bright white gates, each with a large red spot in the centre. These, arranged as a double, made a fairly intimidating sight. From a horse's viewpoint they would have looked like a single gate eight feet tall. Some fences almost beg to be jumped: inviting you in with an uphill approach, wide wings and rustic poles. Others are by design off-putting, to a horse and, by implication, to a rider. This was a fence that would sort out a certain type of horse and a certain type of rider.

I knew the twin fences would be a challenge to Trev, but I also knew that he was perfectly capable of making the height. The previous day he had performed creditably in Grade C: in this all-comers event he had what was necessary to put up a good show.

It was a demanding course but we were clear as we approached the gates. I took a small, steadying pull as we landed from the fence before; rode the line I had walked before the event began, so that we approached the fences without too much time to think about them and yet without springing it on Trev as a surprise. And I got it pretty well right: a good, confident rhythm that made the fence ahead part of the inevitable flow of a good showjumping round. I felt a slight hesitation as we straightened for the fence but I rode strong, not kicking but pushing on with serious purpose, compelling but not bullying. Feel my confidence, Trev: feel it and make it yours.

Trev responded and cantered into the fence with complete commitment. This was great. Perfectly into the rhythm of his take-off stride, I threw myself forward for the jump, rising up his neck – and kept going. And going. Alone.

Even with his forelegs raised to jump, Trev had second thoughts. Stopped on a dime. Half-turned right. I was catapulted from the saddle: it was as if it had turned into a Martin-Baker ejector seat. As I began to soar I was turned round in the air by the twisting nature of Trev's tumultuous halt. It was not Trev that took the jump but me: but alas with a knock-down. I hit the fence arse-first and knocked it over, ended up flat-out on the damn thing as it lay on the floor. Trev looking down in puzzlement: how the hell did *he* get there?

I remounted. They stood the damn gate up again and I tried the fence twice more, as regulations permit, but on neither occasion did we get within a stride of it. Trev knew that the fence bit, and he was having none of it. Three refusals: elimination. So it goes. By the time I had ridden back to Dragon Hall the adrenalin had worn off and the pain began to wear on. The following day my arse was a rainbow.

Two things. The first was that, at this fence, Trev showed me unequivocally where his limits lay. He wasn't good enough to do much more than this. And if there were legitimate doubts about my skills and my courage, there were also doubts about Trev. He was both too old and too inexperienced to take on the further challenges he had been offered. He had neither the boldness that comes with youth, nor the confidence that comes with the right kind of experience. It also comes with the nature of the horse: after all, Trev had been selectively bred to race, not to jump. This second career was in a sense against nature; at any rate against the bloodlines that humans had established in him. We had done all that we could – and it was all very fabulous and I'm deeply grateful for the times we had. This incident was a kind of footnote, an asterisk: and what it meant was that in terms of sporting ambition it was where Trev and I hit the buffers.

The second thing was the nature of the fall. It was absolutely fine. It's the sort of thing that happens when a horse's inadequacies are found out. It's a fall you will see at all levels of showjumping, and it happens when a horse is facing a fence that's a bit beyond his courage, his athletic abilities and/or his experience. In short, when the horse is slightly overfaced. Sometimes the horse stops because the rider has brought the horse in wrong; but sometimes it happens because the horse doesn't have what's required to make the jump.

It was precisely the fall that happened to my dear friend Melanie Reid. I never saw her ride but, at a guess, I'd say she was a bit better than me. Many people will know her for the brilliant column she writes in *The Times*. The problem was that the fall happened to her when she was riding in a cross-country event. The fence she hit was solid. Unforgiving. It didn't give as she struck it. And she is a tetraplegic as a result.

I often think of Mel when I'm around horses. And I'm around horses every day of my life.

# Chapter 32

# Ghost of a Cricketer

My return from Asia to England involved all kinds of radical reappraisals. So many matters needed to be confronted from a new footing: and yet the ghosts of old things, things I thought I had left behind when I set off on my adventures four years earlier, started cropping up again to ask difficult and sometimes dismaying questions.

I got married, we bought a flat, I started to write about sport for *The Times*. And I played cricket. This was a destiny that had been closing in with terrible force as soon as I arrived back in England: the feeling that some kind of accommodation with cricket had to be reached. For some reason it seemed an important matter as I attempted to fit the anomalies of boyhood into the newly established patterns of grown-up life in England. It seemed that I needed to confront once again the crushing disappointments of childhood as I made my long-delayed entrance into adult life.

For I still had, deeply buried, never discussed, seldom even admitted to myself, the belief that I was a cricketer. It was just that I had never played cricket. Not properly. I was, if you like, a Platonic cricketer: I suspect the world is full of Platonic sportsmen and sportswomen: people who see themselves as sportspeople without actually playing sport. I was like that when I wrote about sport on local papers. But now I wanted to get Plato out of it and redefine my sporting philosophy, perhaps with Nietzsche. 'Live dangerously! Build your houses on the slopes of Vesuvius!'

By this time my expectations had been modified. I no longer believed that I would turn into a Test match batsman the instant I buckled on a real pad. But I felt that I ought to be able to play cricket with some kind of basic competence. After all, I was a goalkeeper (think of that save on the golden afternoon) and a competitive horseman (remember that treble). Surely cricket was not beyond me.

The truly odd thing is that my two brothers-in-law were possessed by the same feeling. We had all missed the boat as boy cricketers but we all believed that we could refloat the whole damn daydream in our 30s. We just felt that cricket would sort of come to us.

So there was me, Roob and John, family nickname Salty. Salty, also a journalist, had a gift for bonhomie and organisation and he set up a one-off cricket match, calling on various old friends of his who could actually play, along with the three of us and a couple who came along to make up the numbers. He arranged the hire of a proper cricket pitch, and fixed up opponents, a team called the Daily Mirror Badgers. He was to bat, Roob was to bowl, I was to keep wicket. That none of us could really do these things didn't seem that much of a problem.

When I was travelling in Sri Lanka during one of my jaunts from my base in Hong Kong, I had bought, for a few small coins, a locally printed how-to book by the great wicketkeeper Bob Taylor. It was, on the face of it, an odd thing to do: I wasn't a wicketkeeper and I had no chance of becoming one. I just felt that the book would be a useful thing to have.

So I reread this fine if blurry work, and learned that you always point the fingers down or up: never straight forwards or you'll catch the ball on the end of a finger like a snooker cue and break it. I learned about making my hands into a trawl net, as wide as possible, little fingers linked. And after that it was – well, up to me. Watch the ball. Yes, right. Always watch the ball.

The standard of that match was fair. As always with cricket matches played at this pick-up level, there are a few really good players, a few bluffers like me, and a few who come along for the ride. It was in the course of this match that I made the great discovery that good bowling is easier for a wicketkeeper than bad bowling: even if it's quite quick you know roughly where the ball is going. At least, that's true when standing back to what we humorously called 'fast' bowling. It's harder to keep to a proper spinner because you must stand up to the stumps. Salty had recruited a decent left-armer and I found that he bowled about a foot faster than my own reactions. It was a sad thing to drop the ball with the batsman halfway up the pitch.

Being a wicketkeeper is the one specialist job in cricket that you can do without coaching. Obviously coaching helps, and so does endless practice, but if you are agile and can catch, keeping wicket is within the ambitions of someone who was never been coached and has never practised, in any demanding sense of the term, the skills of cricket. I flailed and I flapped. I dealt properly with some balls that came through, others I dropped. I conceded byes; I stopped a few as well. I didn't do very well, but I wasn't embarrassingly bad.

And there was one ball. Roob bowled it. Lack of coaching and practice meant that his bowling action was always a little haphazard. He lacked what is called 'a grooved action'. He was tall and pretty strong, but the consistency that comes of practice and early training forever eluded him. All the same, you couldn't rely on him to bowl a bad ball every time.

And he got one dead right. On a sluggish pitch in a Hertfordshire village he got the only ball of the day – and there were some decent bowlers around – to jump off a length. This one spat up at the batsman, and he spliced it in a soft loop towards silly point. As there wasn't a silly point I ran half-a-dozen strides and caught it with a bravura dive that would have won me credit among my team-mates at Gwai Loong FC. The batsman gave me and Roob a resigned look, shrugged and walked off.

The Shrug Ball, we called it. Still do, occasionally. What can you *do* with a ball like that?

And despite the intense awareness of my limitations, I loved everything about that day of cricket. It wasn't just the pleasures of playing. There was also a head-spinning sensation of being part of the living mythology of the sport. Being an insider, not an outsider. Being a participant, not an observer. Being part of the same continuum as Bob Taylor and the other names he let slip in the course of the book, names like Ian Botham, Mike Brearley and Bob Willis. I was one of them now.

Sport is in some ways an act of self-definition. I wanted to be the sort of person who played cricket just as much as I wanted to play cricket. I wanted to be part of a team. I wanted to pull on a white cable-knit sweater. I wanted to shout 'how's that'. I watched cricket, I wrote about cricket; and now I wanted to do these things in the knowledge that I, too, was a cricketer.

It wasn't that I wanted to be upsides with the boy cricketer who had failed so abysmally. Rather, I was still possessed by the same thing that had caused me to step on to the cricket field of Sunnyhill School with such unrealistic hopes. I wasn't driving out a ghost; I was bringing the ghost back to haunt me all over again.

# Chapter 33

# Foundation Myth

Cricket loves a meeting. It's perhaps the most committee-laden game in history. There have been many meetings of high and rarefied importance in the history of cricket, meetings that discussed the formalising of the rules, Bodyline, the involvement of newly independent India, the ending of amateurism, the selection of Basil D'Oliveira and the admission of women to the MCC. This was one of their number. It took place in Hill House Road, in Streatham, in what was once my bedroom, in the course of a family party with a borrowed bottle of champagne to help things along. Those present: me, Roob, Salty. To discuss: the foundation of Tewin Irregulars Cricket Club.

It was agreed – though we put it in other words – that we all shared the fantasy of becoming adequate cricketers even in our sporting dotage: that, having missed the experience of playing cricket at a more suitable age, we should give a great deal of time and thought to the creation of a second chance. It was accepted that none of us would get into a proper cricket team – certainly not all together – unless it was our ball. Playground rules would operate. By starting our own team we would become untouchables, in the sporting rather than the Hindu sense of the term. No one could drop us, no one would ever find some other better younger person to take our place.

The next question was opposition. We reckoned that between us we could come up with half a dozen – no more, what about that lot? – teams, some scratch, some playing several times a season. A fixture list would not be a problem.

A ground, then? Roob then lived in the Hertfordshire village of Tewin, which had a cricket ground, and they would hire it to us on days they weren't using it themselves. So the name was obvious, and implied what we hoped was a flattering affiliation to Tewin Cricket Club itself. I'm not sure they saw it quite like that, especially as the team acquired a certain notoriety. Roob, we agreed, would be captain, Salty his deputy.

But the big question remained. How could we – we as a team rather than as individual aspirants for cricketing glory – possibly be any good? We all knew people who played cricket and who might turn out for us now and then, but we needed some sort of scaffolding of excellence on which to build the side. Salty thought he had the answer to this overwhelming question. 'Fish,' he said. 'I think Chris would probably play too. But if Fish agrees to turn out – well, we're sorted.'

And that was unarguable. Fish – Paul Fisher – had played in the Shrug Ball game; one of those big men who learned early in life that their physical size means they never have to show a moment of aggression to anyone. He was a man of softly spoken, witty remarks. He was heavy on the irony, always alive to absurdity. And behind that he had a very clear idea of what cricket – what village green cricket – should be. It was a kind of moral vision. You could assemble it from warm beer, the sound of turtle doves, chestnut trees in flower, white-clad figures on a green background, run-stealers flickering to and fro, to and fro; yet with a certain artisan spirit, requiring a boisterous rejection of pomposity and a thoroughly modern inclusiveness that is deeply English without being at all insular, still less racist.

It was also about playing hard in the certainty that in the end it didn't really matter. And it was about tolerance for a wide range of ability and the necessity for decent behaviour to opponents. Above all, it was about the way in which Fish made us all co-conspirators: keepers of a shared secret. This secret was that this daft and often painful game was at base a profound source of merriment and joy – and above all it was there to be shared. 'He can cricket,' I once overheard Fish saying. And he was talking about me. What more need I say?

I had enjoyed keeping to Fish's bowling in the Shrug Ball game. He ran up with a sort of rhythmic shamble: the business end of the action was all from the shoulders, the pace always a little sharper than you'd expect from the benign run-up. He was accurate too, so that the ball tended to come to your gloves rather than send you searching for it, and when he did slip one down the leg side, it still tended to be on a length, which made things a good deal easier. The ball slammed into my borrowed gloves and stung my palms but I reckoned that my timing would improve with use.

Yes. Me out there, crouching low, rising as he released the ball, my hands spread out wide as a trawl net, the better to catch Fish, little fingers linked, taking the ball slap – the *mot juste*, alas – in the middle of the net, where the edges of my palms were pressed hard together.

I wasn't worried about winning and losing. I just wanted to be out there, dressed in white, feeling the ball in my gloves, occasionally shouting 'how's that' or 'bowled, Fish!'. I wanted to play cricket, yes, but, more than that, I wanted to be a cricketer. And now I was.

# Chapter 34

# The Real Thing

Village cricket isn't funny to villagers. Words of the great John Arlott. You have to be serious about sport, at some relatively profound level. Or it isn't sport. Not humourless. Just serious. Serious *enough*. As Tewin Irregulars established themselves as a cricket team with a real fixture list, it became clear that this kind of cricket is as serious in its way as a Test match.

I understood very early on that there are two types of personality unsuited to cricket at this level. The first is the player who takes it all with white-faced life-and-death desperation; the second is the person who is having a laugh, just messing about, three pints before the match and who gives a toss. It's a fine balance, but it's essential. It's also readily attainable: serious yet not serious. Playing village cricket gets right to the heart of sport's essential paradox: it's a triviality that can only exist if you take it seriously. Fish was the massive embodiment of this principle in action. Nobody could face his bowling without being aware of sport's serious nature; nobody could remain in his company for long without sharing his relish for the absurd nature of the proceedings.

I should at this point explain something of the nature of this kind of cricket. There isn't really a name for it: I called it village cricket because we mostly played in Hertfordshire villages, usually Tewin. Those that play cricket in leagues call it picnic cricket or (worse) social cricket. It's not unsociable, but the object of the occasion is to play hardball and to try to win.

Neither we nor our opponents were affiliated to an organisation with a formal structure. We had no responsibilities to a league or an association. Our responsibilities were, I suppose, to the greater glory of sport. Teams played each other by mutual agreement, not because someone told us to. And if we didn't like 'em, we usually dropped the fixture.

The week before the match was always fraught for both teams. It would all be about the telephone: call after call as we tried to assemble 11 men. Preferably cricketers. By Friday night, that bloke you never much liked but for some reason you seem to have his phone number – hell, give him a call even if he's never played the bloody game in his life. As the Irregulars established themselves as part of the cricketing landscape, many of the more agreeable players from our opponents would be invited to play for us; many of them accepted, only to become implacable enemies when we next encountered them. It's fair to say that these matches were frequently won and lost on the phone.

Once play began, members of the batting team would take turns to umpire and keep the score. The home team would supply a tea: this often meant (my brothers-in-law and I took turns) a Saturday evening of mad boiling of eggs after a trolley-dash round the supermarket for sliced bread and random cakes.

The format of the match was crucial. It was just a game of bloody cricket, as we liked to say. None of your limited-overs nonsense: real cricket, in which all four results were possible, a draw being an essential part of the dynamic of the game. The team that batted first was, if not bowled out, under a moral obligation to declare in time for tea. Afterwards they were required to bowl 20 overs after six o'clock.

We needed to be respectable. A proper cricket team with proper cricketers in it. We opened the bowling with Fish at one end and Chris at the other. Chris, from Yorkshire, dark, stocky and with almost unreasonable breadth of shoulder, was built on the lines of Fred Trueman. He had a long, beautifully rhythmic run-up and was a shade faster than Fish; I was, after all, in the best possible position to know that. I could measure the pace by the sting in my gloves. Still, perhaps I would start timing the ball better soon: giving with my gloves as the ball struck, so that it entered as silently as a rabbit diving into a hole. Instead of that horrible slap.

Serious, as I say, but serious in the right way. Which brings us to Mart. He played for a team – well, I don't want any bad vibes about cricket long since played, so I'll call them the Fleet Street Undesirables. Mart had become a standing joke among Tewin Irregulars because he refused to walk when clean-bowled. After Fish had rearranged his stumps somewhat, he stood there, holding the pose for the cameras with his hands on his hips, staring back at the bowler. He then lowered his head like a bloodhound and walked slowly forward, eyes on the pitch. Suddenly he stopped still, as if he had received a small electric shock. And then he wagged his head and gave out a short bitter laugh while banging the toe-end of his bat into the offending place on the pitch. Finally, sadly, but resigned to the world's injustice, he turned and set off for the pavilion. Fish said softly as he went: 'It actually deviated off the seam, Mart. Do you want come back and bang that?'

A year later, there was high excitement as the Undesirables made their return to Tewin. Eventually Mart came out to bat. 'It's him!' I said to the slips and gully fielders. 'It's Mart! The one who didn't walk when clean-bowled. Let's see if he does it again!'

He did.

It was rather wonderful. Either Fish or Chris got him before he had scored. Mart turned around through 180 degrees and looked at me and the fielders standing alongside, all of us giggling in delight. 'And next time … I want no talking in the slips!'

This was my second full season as a wicketkeeper and I was adequately prepared for the conversational efforts that are sometimes required from this position. I pointed out – politely enough – that the ball had hit the stumps and that under the conventions of cricket he was required to return to the pavilion. Thus perish all sportsmen who fail to understand sport.

At moments like this I wondered if sport had been designed to be played with the aching intensity that comes at the very highest level. Top-level sport requires adults to play a children's game – and to do so as if their lives depended on it. It sometimes seems that the structure of sport is inadequate for this mighty load.

That's why at many major sporting events we have all kinds of technology to measure the decisions. Hawk-Eye, used in tennis and cricket to record (and in some cases to predict) the flight of the ball was developed from missile-tracking technology and techniques used in brain surgery, for God's sake.

Cricket was invented as a game to be played without reference to missiles. Making cricket – or any other sport – the entire purpose and meaning of your life is a relatively modern departure, no older than half a century. It began with professionalism and took hold as television revenues turned sport into business.

You can see top-level sport bend and sometimes break under the strain of it all. A passer-by who stopped on one of the benches that surrounded Tewin Green might think that this was a pale shadow of proper cricket: as far from a Test match as Tewin is from Sydney Cricket Ground. But sometimes I wondered if that match on Tewin Green, played with a good heart, a proper level of commitment, a decent level of generosity and a small whiff of irony, didn't in fact represent not only the best form of the game but the true form of the game. Perhaps Test match cricket is the distortion. Perhaps it's the game played on the village green that's real.

## Chapter 35

# Sport's Dreamtime

Dreams. An inextricable part of sport, some say. But I've never been happy with that word in the sporting context. I'm reminded of the Island where Dreams come true: a place approached by the crew of the *Dawn Treader* in *The Chronicles of Narnia*.

'I reckon I'd find I was married to Nancy if we landed here.'

'And I'd find Tom alive again,' said another.

'Fools!' said the man, stamping his foot with rage. 'That is the sort of talk that brought me here, and I'd better have been drowned or never been born. Do you hear what I say? This is where dreams – dreams, do you understand – come real. Not daydreams – dreams.'

The real sporting dream is not of victory and joy and adulation. It's more like walking naked into an airport with your legs glued together knowing you have only minutes to catch your flight, with an exam in some unrevised subject waiting for you once you get on board.

Sport is like a dream in that it is quite separate from normal waking life, and is frequently absurd, pointless, terrifying, incoherent, nasty and humiliating. It's not very often like a daydream of perfection in which everything you've ever wanted is there for the taking. Sometimes when I hear people talking about their 'dreams' it seems to me as if they are talking about their rights; as if eternal happiness was the birthright of all humans. To believe that is surely to embrace misery and failure as your lot. Never mind: a little serious sport will soon disabuse you of that notion.

So let me tell you about some of my sporting dreams that have come real. Dropping a sharp but straightforward chance off Fish's bowling and the batsman went on to win the match for them. Batting for Mrs Holland's class. Letting in a stupid goal. Losing at ping-pong when leading 19–12 in the last set. Worst of all, that attack of rather bad peritonitis that routinely afflicted me on the start line of cross-country events.

All of sport's pleasures must be understood in the context of that sort of dream. The rare moments of achievement stand out in sharp contrast from the background of terrible dreams: and that has to be true at every level at which sport is played, for even champions are hag-ridden by failure and doubt. Even for the greatest, sport is never easy. Even the greatest find that the pleasures of sport are paid for in the hard currency of disappointment and fear. I always think of Ian Botham when I think about self-confidence in sport: for he is a man who seems never to have had a moment of doubt in his life. And then I remember the day he resigned as England captain in 1981, his face the colour of sour cream, unshed tears in his eyes. His resurgence was one of the great sporting tales, but you seldom rise again to glory without first tasting a little hell.

If you are prepared to pay the price – and the only price is failure – there will be other days. One of the great pleasures for all those who played for Tewin Irregulars was the way that, along with the routine humiliations and disappointments, sport handed most of the regular participants something to treasure, albeit foolishly, for the rest of our lives. Daydreams, in the married-to-Nancy sense of the term, are available in sport, even if they don't come as a right. Dreams of the everyday fearful kind come along in packs like the 49 bus, but that doesn't mean that daydreams are entirely beyond your reach.

Tim was almost as regular an Irregular as I was, and he played for not dissimilar reasons. He normally came on to bowl first or second change: tall, bowling seam-up trundlers. He was always aware that he wasn't a proper bowler, in the sense that Fish and Chris were. This was inclined to make him self-conscious, and occasionally prone to the yips: that nervous affliction in which you find yourself unable to perform the routine tasks of sport. Tim sometimes had difficulty letting go of the ball. On one of these occasions, he dropped the ball in his delivery stride two balls running. At the third attempt the ball trickled to the batsman, not quite reaching him. The batsman was nearing his 50, having played Fish and Chris with immense competence, and he was taking the game away from us. He failed to deal with Tim's troubles sympathetically; he practically spat on the ball. So Tim made a huge effort with his next ball – and this time released it too soon. It rose in a steepling arc, the biggest lushest rankest full toss in the history of cricket. The batsman took a mighty swing at it. And missed. The ball landed on the bails.

But there was one occasion when such joyous farce seemed quite alien to the bowler I was keeping to. Tim, forced into the role of strike bowler by the absence of Fish and Chris, was suddenly twice the cricketer. Freed from the shackles of self-consciousness he was at least a couple of yards quicker, getting bounce from his height and real accuracy. It was Tim Unbound. He took five wickets and won the match for us.

His uncle played for us many times. Years before, David had run his own version of Tewin Irregulars – Wilder's Waggoners – though it was always implied, in a gentlemanly fashion, that the Waggoners' standard of cricket was a couple of notches higher. David always fielded at first slip, not because he was likely to catch anything, but because his years precluded too much running about. He was supreme in that position, maintaining a non-stop flood of spiky comments audible only to me, about the batsmen, the deficiencies of our own team and many other important matters. He also played a fine game in the pub afterwards, though he turned too often for my comfort to the great trauma of his sporting life. This had occurred when he was tried for Surrey and was found wanting. His rejection was brutal: it still stung even though he had sought comfort in a thousand matches on a thousand village greens.

He always batted with a studied elegance, strong on the cut, rolling the wrists over the ball in a well-coached fashion. Alas, by the time he was playing for us he tended to play these shots a fraction after the ball was gone. He made a series of rather stylish single-figure scores. No bar to selection that, obviously. But there was one afternoon when he started middling the ball. He was in the late 20s, or perhaps even early 30s, when Roob, watching with me from the pavvy, said: 'Oh God, wouldn't it be marvellous if David got a 50.' David was unable to hear the remark, of course, but it was enough to do for him next ball. Still, he walked off to great and affectionate applause, and raised his bat modestly as if he did such a thing every week.

Then there was a Catholic priest called Bernard, an amiable, uncoordinated man without any sporting gifts of any kind. He played regularly for us for a couple of seasons and it was always good to have him around. One afternoon he was fielding at gully, no idea why because he was no crash-hot fielder. The batsman hit a ball off the face of the bat: and there was Bernard diving full length to his right and taking the ball one-handed an inch above the grass. It was a screamer. A catch that would have had many a replay in a Test match. It was way beyond his normal capacity: yet he still had this moment of greatness within him. From my place behind the stumps I could see the expression on his face as he rolled over: undiluted astonishment.

Or Gerry, an actor and a fast(ish) bowler, who famously announced after one spell: 'I have Nothing Left to Give.' On one occasion, Salty, filled with delusions of captaincy, asked him to open the batting, in the belief that he would find solidity and responsibility in such a task. He was out for 28 in the third over of the match.

Or my father, bowling against us for BBC Children's Programmes (he went on to become head of that department), taking wickets with his looping leg-breaks; he would have had a hat-trick if the wicketkeeper – not me, let me stress – had had the presence of mind to remove the bails and stump the batsman with the third devastating ball, instead of waving the ball about and appealing.

Or anybody, really, even me. There is a greatness of a kind within us all: moments when the least likely of us come across the tiniest scruple of ability. Sometimes, like monkeys and Shakespeare, it seems to come about as a result of the time invested: if you play for Tewin Irregulars often enough, then your turn for one of those little moments of delight must come along eventually. But the thing to concentrate on here is that if you take delight in sport, you have something in you that responds to the doing of it. As all the cricketers just mentioned have found out: for there will be times when you play better than you do normally.

That's true for all sporting performers, even the greatest. 'It's a double-edged sword,' Graham Gooch, former England cricket captain once told me. 'You play well because you're playing well; you play badly just because you're playing badly.'

For some of us, playing badly is the norm: playing adequately is the attainable goal. And every so often, you play a little better than that: and it feels like nothing less than greatness. Even though you know it's nothing of the kind. It's great by your standards though, and that's enough to be going on with. And enough to be recollected in private moments years and years after the catch stuck, the wickets fell, the boundaries were struck.

# Chapter 36

# Perfect Dolores

For some men sport is a kind of shed, a place where they can get away from women, children and household tasks. I suspect this reflects the earliest human societies. They weren't really about the Man the Hunter: they were about Woman the Gatherer. The women did the important jobs of food-finding and nurturing while the men skived off and played sport. Sometimes to be rewarded with a great protein bonanza, because the sport in question was hunting. And sometimes they returned with nothing, but, as we've seen already in these pages, losing is as much a part of sport as the other thing.

There is a kind of man who believes that life is less serious, less meaningful, when there are women around, though I have never seen life in this way myself. And for all that mighty Gwai Loong and the equally mighty Tewin Irregulars were all-male things, I have never seen sport as a blokes-only business. As I competed on horseback in Hong Kong I faced female instructors, female administrators, female opponents and female victors. 'Well ridden,' I had to say when a chit of a girl won the red ribbon instead of me. And back in England I returned to the world of the horsey sports and had to accept right from the start that I would be regularly beaten by schoolgirls.

I bought a fabulously talented if deeply flawed little mare. She was called Dolly Dolores VII and in her company I threw myself wholeheartedly into the horsey life of England. She was a step up from Favour and Trev: after all, she was bred and trained as a jumper. She was small, strong, possessed of an immense jump and a reckless and impetuous nature. It was an instant click: and, for all the fine times I had with the Irregulars, it was with Dolores that I found my deepest sporting joys. Not entirely by coincidence, I think, it was because Dolores and I were quite good at the level we competed. That is to say, local shows: anyone can turn up, pay entry money and take part.

I went to these events with a gaggle of very loud, very cockney and very lovely horsey ladies. We all kept our horses at the same yard – Jan's place – somewhere in darkest Hertfordshire. There was not much money around, and what there was went on horses: horses are not just for the wealthy. The horsey joys are there for anyone who wants to make horses a priority.

It took me a while to get the hang of Dolores. She was more horse than I had ever sat on before, both in terms of her ability and her approach. In the early days I rode her too pedantically, as if I was still riding Trev and had to explain to him in detail about every fence as we approached it. I had to learn to back off with Dolores: to understand when she needed input from me and when she didn't. She didn't like micro-management. I tried in the early days to get something smooth and controlled and got the exact opposite: a round of constant stop-go: check, check, give, jump, check again.

So it was a process of learning to trust. It wasn't hard: in all the time I rode her I never once knew her to refuse a fence. I had some lovely horses before, and for that matter after Dolores: but she was, beyond question, the horse of my life. But this is a book about sport, not about horses, so we'll move on. And I'll tell you about a day of sporting perfection.

It was perfect in the way that an Islamic carpet is perfect. The weaver of the carpet puts in a deliberate flaw to show that he has no ambition to rival God. Here the flaw was not deliberate at all, but it made the afternoon a more vivid experience than you could get from the pure symmetry of perfection.

It was a foul day in early February. The rain was horizontal. The action took place in one of those chilled and joyless indoor buildings in which equestrian disciplines can be pursued in all weathers. We were showjumping, four of us from Jan's place. A surprising number of riders from other yards had turned up to try their luck that day. The competitive action took place in the dry: everything else happened outside in the merciless rain. The warm-up ring, then, was not overly warm. There was a person at the big double doors of the arena who would kindly take your waterproof before you entered, and then you found yourself in a cramped arena crowded with jumps.

You need to be very accurate indeed in these circumstances. You need your horse to keep balanced and composed without losing speed and power. You need to be able to turn at precisely the spot you choose and hit a stride at once, for there is no room for last-minute corrections. You need a horse with the ability to make very tight turns without losing the will and ability to jump. A pretty fair description of Dolores.

So I entered three competitions, novice, intermediate and open, that's to say, low fences, medium fences and fences that required a serious jump. And we jumped four rounds without touching a pole: two double-clears, and if we didn't win it was because I didn't go for the jump-off with enough conviction. In each there was one or two better, but I still got placed. It was my friends from Jan's yard who did the winning, as things turned out, because we were all on fire that day. It was like a team thing, even though we weren't on the field of play at the same time and we weren't actually in a team event. It just felt that way: and so each person's success led to the next person's success, and we were all very joyful about it.

It's the open event I remember best. It was probably the best round of showjumping I rode in my life. It was a little beyond our normal scope, but that only added to the pleasures of it. I felt my concentration as a finely honed thing: perfect for the task ahead. Nothing existed outside this strange little space, the rain hammering on the corrugated-iron roof above our heads. Dolores was both keyed up and relaxed, listening to me without tension, but with immense eagerness. We were united. Damn it, we were perfect.

When fences reach a certain height, you have to jump them properly. A horse can scramble over low fences, or hurdle them in a long, raking stride, but there comes a height at which the only way to get over a fence is to make a big arch. It's all in the shape: a horse must *bascule* over it, as showjumping people say. This was not a course you could muddle through: you had to get the approach right, jump right, land right, and in your landing stride be already locked on to the next fence and fully committed, because in this crowded space it was coming up pretty damn quick. That's why, in action shots of showjumping, you often see a rider looking hard right or left as the horse lands – to make that turn as the logical outcome of the jump, so that each jump is an integral part of the jump before. Smoothness, rhythm: a pattern of logic measured out in strides.

Dolores and I jumped each fence in sequence in the unearthly silence of this intimate little arena: the triple-beat of her hooves on the woodchip beneath them, the sound of her staccato breaths as she exerted herself to get each jump right, tucking up her front hooves to her belly to keep them clear of the poles, flicking up her back hooves on the descent to avoid dragging them down into the fence.

One. And two. And three. And the double with a great bounding inevitable rhythm: annihilating all that's made to a pole and a stride and a horse and me.

I knew enough not to ease up as we went into the last fence. We met it on a very good stride, and I could feel the coiled power of her as she went into her bascule: flowing over it like a Slinky toy descending a staircase.

I can hear it still.

'Ahhhhh.'

A great sigh of disappointment torn involuntarily from the chests of the 30 or 40 spectators in the gallery: the empathy that unites humans, that makes us yawn when another yawns and cough when another coughs. Here was disappointment shared and made audible. And at the same moment the soft musical clunk of a falling pole: a gamelan note of woe.

It's possible to hit a showjumping fence with immense force and get away with it, the pole bouncing capriciously back into the cups that held it. And it's equally possible to caress a pole from the cups: to roll it out gently, wafting it with a touch like a feather and persuading it to tumble to the ground and sound its single note of doom.

We did the second of these things. Carefully, almost pedantically, we rolled the pole from its cups and nudged it to the ground, and so our day was at an end.

Dolores just didn't make the height, probably because this was her fifth round of the day and she never gave anything in half-measure. Or perhaps I got her a fraction too close to the fence. Either way, we had done the best we were capable of: and there is a very deep satisfaction in that. I was made aware of my – of our – limitations, which is a powerful experience, but on the other hand, the limits of our performance were higher than I had realised. So I was happy and I was sad: I was a loser and I was a winner: I was a good rider and I was a bad rider. I was not as good as I hoped: but better than I ever thought I would be.

# Chapter 37

# Eddy Pratt

Eddy Pratt was an amateur banker and a professional sportsman. Admittedly he got paid for his work for one of the High Street banks and no one ever gave him a cent for playing sport, but it was to sport that he devoted the best of his working life and the serious part of his mind. There was a time when we were next-door neighbours and most weeks we would go out to the Two Brewers and argue about sport.

We espoused antithetical points of view. He would hymn the beauties of George Graham's Arsenal: of defensive discipline, of the 1–0 victory. I would speak out in favour of Glenn Hoddle and an approach based on romanticism: the search for some kind of transcendental glory. 'I could watch Glenda all day long; I wouldn't cross the road to watch your Arsenal boys.'

'That's because you know nothing about sport. They're not doing it for you. You're nothing to do with it. They're trying to win football matches.'

'But the game's about glory, doing it in style, as Danny Blanch—'

'The game's about winning. All games are. Whatever way you can. If you can't play like Hoddle you don't try to: you play like Tony Adams. Sport's not supposed to be about entertainment. You can go to the pictures if you want entertainment ...'

Eddy had played football. He had also played a fair amount of rugby at fly-half for his old school. He played cricket for the old boys for years. He was now devoting himself to golf and his ambition – long elusive, eventually realised – to play off a single-figure handicap. 'You don't think a sport should have some element of physical risk about it then, Eddy ...'

It was inevitable, then, that Eddy should turn out for Tewin Irregulars. His two sons, Giles and Jason, sometimes played as well. Jason was a landscape gardener; at my suggestion he called his firm Capability Pratt. I loved keeping wicket to Eddy: you just put your gloves out behind the off stump and the ball would hit them. He bowled seam-up in-duckers at what counted on Tewin Green as medium pace. He was canny, highly competitive and extremely accurate. He had one significant variation: every now and then he would turn and bowl off two paces, at which I would step back a pace and half, because that was his quicker one.

Keeping to Eddy against almost any opposition was about as good as it got for me on the cricket field. I could be certain, confident, almost precise when Eddy was bowling. It felt like a double act: as if we had the batsman caught in a pincer movement. Our unison appeal for an lbw was a fine thing, audible in the village called Tewin Wood, perhaps even in Welwyn Garden City. It was a rare thing for a batsman to take a liberty with him; he was machine-accurate, the atmosphere always crackling with competitiveness, even if there was always the right amount of joshing between overs. I remember one duel he had with a very good batsman who was closing in on a century when he drove a little early at one that Eddy held back. Eddy took a diving catch, one-handed, at the very boots of the non-striker. It was the only time I ever saw him dive.

One winter we decided to do winter nets: Eddy and his boys, me and Eddy's brother-in-law, Jeremy. We did this for four or five years running, from January to April: at Hatfield, Finchley, and at the Alf Gover Cricket School in Wandsworth.

I was nervous about this because it involved batting. That is to say, 15 minutes of solid batting – Eddy only ever bowled – against bowling that was very accurate – Eddy and Giles – and pretty damn quick – Giles and Jason. If you have ever wanted to know how it feels to be a skittle in a bowling alley, try indoors nets: half a dozen nets going at once, with the thumps and clunks echoing in the high-ceilinged space, and a ball coming at you every 20 seconds or so.

I was pretty hopeless at first. I had never been examined so long and so relentlessly as a batsman. I had muddled through, sometimes scoring a few runs with my cut shot, a kind of petulant slap square of the wicket. But accuracy and pace tended to find me out pretty quickly: and accuracy and pace was precisely what I got in the nets. At one establishment the stumps were made from metal pipes, and when they were struck they leapt from their sockets and clattered about the floor, ringing out like a fire alarm. I was once bowled in three successive balls by three successive Pratts: it sounded like the final frenzies of *Tubular Bells*. 'Not ideal, Simon,' Jason said. Only one real prat in this net, then.

I had never practised a ball game in this manner: concentrated, repetitive, unrelenting. There was no coaching, so it was a question of trying to work out a method. And I have to confess that the method I came up with had more in common with Tony Adams and George Graham than it did with Glenn Hoddle and Danny Blanchflower. I didn't go looking for glory. I went out there to stop those Pratts hitting my wicket. I wasn't good enough to cause them pain but I could surely get good enough to bugger them up.

And slowly I did so. Eddy occasionally found my limitations with the extravagant swing he could get in an indoor net, especially when he doctored a ball with lip salve. Giles was the quickest but the most straightforward. I worked out a trigger movement: a small shuffle from leg to off, towards middle of the stumps. This was to encourage me to get in line rather than back off, a natural instinct but a wrong one for both sport and self-respect. Jason's unpredictability was a lot harder to deal with: he would send wides and full tosses but mix them up with balls that stood up off a length and others that trimmed the top of off stump.

I also had to bowl. I soon began to enjoy this. I settled on the non-turning off-break as a stock ball: tossed high and bowled full. This could be varied with the one that goes straight on with the arm. I would try an occasional leg-break: this actually turned. At any rate it did on the occasions when it hit the ground before reaching the batsman. My line tended to be bit variable with the leg-spinner, but I could mostly put the stock ball where

I wanted to. It was quite hard for Giles and Jeremy to put it away, and that was a quiet but considerable joy. Jason, having little respect for orthodoxy, tended to hammer it, but even he occasionally missed one and rang the bells for me.

Afterwards we would drink beer and talk about sport. I was becoming a better sportsman. A fraction more professional in the way I thought, and that's a concept that has nothing to do with money. I was a little less spontaneous, a little more purposeful, a good deal more organised. I knew what I could do and what I couldn't: and I had found a way to play within these stifling limitations. As a result I began to watch sport in a fuller, more rounded way.

I stopped waiting to be entertained: I began waiting to be enthralled. Sport is richer and deeper than mere entertainment. I began to understand that if you can't find something interesting about a great champion, the failing is not in him but in you. Thus, years later, when everyone was criticising Pete Sampras for his relentless and 'boring' style of play, I became his champion. I still maintain that Sampras's three-set demolition of Andre Agassi in the 1999 Wimbledon final was the greatest tennis match – and one of the greatest bits of sport – I have ever seen. It was machine-tooled brilliance. I doubt if Roger Federer in his pomp could have lived with Sampras that day, on a court that fast and with equipment of that vintage.

I loved those sessions in the indoor nets, under the artificial lights, the echoing sounds, the serious groups, four or five to each net. What I learned there affected both my professional and my non-professional life. Thanks to Eddy I was able to write about sport and to play sport better than I did before. With greater understanding, with greater purpose, with greater efficiency.

# Chapter 38

# Death of a Wicketkeeper

It was the Amstrad PCW that finished me as a wicketkeeper. Perhaps you, dear reader, also struggled with that primordial piece of computing equipment: a dark screen that glowed eerily with illuminated green script. It was a home word processor, retailing at £399 plus VAT, and among its many quirks and limitations was the fact that the screen gave you no clue whatsoever about how your work would look when you printed it out. Words like Locoscript and Protext may stir long-dormant memories in readers of a certain age.

The truth was that I was never quite as good at keeping wicket as I had hoped. I was fine. At my best, I was OK. But I was never good. I was never consistent. My ambition, never realised, was to go through a match without conceding a bye. Always behind me there seemed to be that fine third man: not a long-stop, not quite, but the clearing up of my errors was clearly – perhaps even ostentatiously – part of his job description.

Not that every ball that passed me was entirely my fault: there was plenty of erratic bowling to go with my erratic wicketkeeping. And I had many good moments. Roob gave up bowling erratic seamers and started to bowl erratic leg-spinners: I pulled off a few memorable stumpings from his looping deliveries. When Fish or Chris was in a good rhythm I could mostly help to keep it going with clean takes and plenty of volume. But I was never better than OK, and that saddened me.

But then came the summer of 1988 in which I produced three books. For the record, these were *A Sportswriter's Year*, a fascinating book all about me, a compilation of journalism under the title *Sportswriter's Eye*, and a collection of literary parodies on a cricketing theme, called *A la Recherche du Cricket Perdu*. All this was better for my literary than my sporting career. This was because the resulting hours I spent staring into the great green cavern of the screen affected my eyes and perhaps my brain. I had two successive matches in which I literally couldn't catch the ball. It was awful: I would get my hands in the way, but all vestige of timing had gone, and I would spill it. Every single time. On the first occasion I was playing an evening match for another team – the Victoria and Albert Museum, as it happened – but their genial captain Nicky Bird wouldn't listen to my request to be replaced behind the stumps, believing I would somehow play myself out of trouble.

Roob adopted the same ploy when I made the same request in a Tewin Irregulars match, and with the same result. When the match was over I placed my pads and my gauntlets – beloved symbols of my life as a cricketer – into the team bag rather than my own. It was a solemn moment, at least for me. I never kept wicket again.

So I reinvented myself as a bowler, taking those non-turning off-breaks out on to the front line. I tended to come on as second or third change and bowl half-a-dozen overs. And to begin with I did all right. I remember bowling against the Badgers when they were going hard at it for a teatime declaration: and their best batsman couldn't hit me off the square. For the first time I understood that old bowler's cliché: I had the ball on a string. I placed it where I wanted to: full, but not driveable, and on a line with off stump. They finished their innings a little short of where they wanted to be: and I thought I had cracked it.

Then came the match against the RSPB. By this time I was writing about wildlife as well as sport, and so I was able to set up this fixture. We played away from Hertfordshire, at a ground of their choosing not far from the RSPB headquarters at Sandy, Bedfordshire, and, as usual for away matches, we struggled to get a decent team. We had one very good batsman, an imposing, rather silent individual named Jim. The rest of us were unexceptional.

As a result of this shortfall in talent I was asked to bowl first change. To step up, in short: to show that I was the real thing. It was the great opportunity of my new life as a bowler. And I wasn't up to it. The fact that we were playing against people I wanted to impress didn't help. But mostly it was the promotion: the sense of being exposed. And I got the yips. Far worse than Tim did on that never-to-be-forgotten day. The occasion overwhelmed me and I was unable to do for real what I had done so often and so well in practice.

At the pace I bowled, a little inaccuracy goes a long way. I had to be very accurate indeed to get away with the stuff I bowled: and accuracy was what I lost. I no longer had it on a string. If anything, I had it on a length of knicker elastic. No control at all, no idea where the next ball was going to go. And it went everywhere and at that pace everything about it said hit me. And hit me they did. I remember overhearing one of the batsman, Trevor, a man a decade older than I was, panting to his batting partner: 'I feel like I've woken to find a 17-year-old nymphomaniac in bed with me, and I just wish I could do proper justice to the occasion.'

They made their teatime declaration at plenty for not very many, and I was pretty disconsolate. So when they requested a substitute fielder, I was happy to volunteer. It was better to have a job to do than sit about thinking about bowling. It was the custom at such matches that if a team was short of players, or one of them had to leave for some reason, the opposition would supply a fielder, to be changed every so often throughout the innings. So I ran on and was asked to field at first slip. I took my place alongside Trevor, who was keeping wicket.

The game progressed and our star batsman Jim came out to bat. He played himself in with some care, but clearly fancied the bowling. He hit a couple of powerful shots and I began to think that we might do better in this match than I had feared.

Then the bowler got one ball to leap off a length. It was certainly the ball of the day. It caught the shoulder of Jim's bat a little below the level of his own shoulder and fizzed off behind the wicket. Straight over Trevor's head; I was vaguely aware of his gauntlets reaching vainly for the ball.

And there was I more or less in the position of leg slip, flat on my back with the ball in my hand. I had dived behind Trevor's back, caught the ball two-handed, goalkeeper-style, with my body parallel to the ground, and then rolled a fair bit. It was the best catch I ever took on a cricket field and it was enough to end the hopes of my own team. I'm told that a bat was thrown with some force shortly after that, but I stayed where I was. I wasn't going back to my own team in any great hurry. Jim never played for us again: but, hell, what was I supposed to do? Drop it?

So there was cricket, there was sport, in all its cruelty, in all its generosity, all its potential for black farce. I recall that catch in immense detail to this day, yet another of those psychokinetic memories. I can also feel the shame and horror of that ruinous spell of bowling; I remember the emotional details of the bowling as precisely as I can remember the physical details of the catch. It was one of those sporting memories associated with the Island where Dreams come true. Not daydreams: dreams.

So I had lost cricket. I lost wicketkeeping to literature and the Amstrad, I lost bowling to my own sense of inadequacy. I carried on for another season or two, but it was never the same. All sporting careers end in disappointment, even if, like Pete Sampras or Steve Redgrave, you go out a winner. You may go out with a medal round your neck, but you're still defeated: Time 1, Athlete 0.

But I had been a cricketer. That was true enough: and among the ruins of my cricketing career the archaeologist could, if sufficiently diligent, find shards and fragments of glory. And that will have to be enough.

# Chapter 39

# Match Drawn

An idyll. Of a kind. A classic English cricket ground at Stonor in the Chilterns: Stonor Park stood opposite, the big house set about with glorious undulating parkland. You could watch the deer on the hill while batting. The ground was surrounded by mature trees. True, the wicket was a bit dodgy, but that was a small price to pay for such visual luxuriance. If you ever fantasised about playing rural cricket in England, this was the ground on which you saw yourself scoring your century, hitting the village blacksmith for six, making the catch that saved the day for the squire's 11.

But this wasn't Hertfordshire, so we were weak that day: as poor a team as Tewin Irregulars ever fielded, though the competition for that accolade is pretty intense. No Fish, no Chris, no Eddy. No batters, certainly not Jim. We were playing the Victoria and Albert Museum; this time I was playing against them rather than for them. It was apparent early on that Nicky had had much better luck than us with the midweek telephoning. All his finest ex-public school champions had turned out that day: a phenomenal bunch of well-coached cricketers with all kinds of lofty cricketing experience.

A score above 150 normally wins the match in this kind of cricket. They declared on 240 for four. It was slaughter. One of their number, wearing an insolent pair of shorts, scored a century and then played a switch-hit. I made my displeasure quite clear: it seemed to me that he was showboating, mocking us to our faces, though now I suspect that the poor fellow was actually trying to get out, in his polite way, and failing.

I came out to bat when we were 80 for eight in reply and we were not very far at all into the 20 overs that had to be bowled before completion. It was all over: time for the last rites. At the other end was Marcus, a colleague from *The Times* and a man with a deep, almost religious belief in cricket as a thing of meaning and beauty. Just about the first thing I did was call him for a run, not because we needed it but because it was such a long single that it seemed churlish not to take it. It turned out that I had misjudged things badly, making my ground with one of my better dives. Marcus and I then had a mid-pitch conference.

'Perhaps it would be better if we didn't run.'

'My thoughts exactly.'

'So you take that end and I'll take this end.'

'See you at close of play.'

So we batted. We blocked. They threw their best bowlers at us and we defied them. It was like being in the indoor nets, except that the ball was less likely to behave properly on this track. But there I was, performing my trigger-movement shuffle into line, getting behind the ball and dropping it at my feet, or pushing forward studiously in the manner of a man defusing a bomb or, most satisfyingly of all, lifting my bat out of the way and letting the ball pass outside off stump. My leave shot was effortlessly the best in my limited vocabulary.

There was a wonderful sense of being besieged, of being surrounded by enemies, and it was a powerful stimulus. I wasn't going to last the course, but damned if you're going to get me this ball. The one after can take care of itself, but I'd die rather than let you get me out this ball.

And then at the non-striker's end I watched Marcus going through the same thing. His face was ready for merriment at most times, but now there was a funereal seriousness about him. We didn't talk much, for fear of breaking the spell, but we exchanged a muttered 'well played' every so often between overs. The spell of sport was upon us: the sense of responsibility was both crushing and inspiring. As the overs ticked down so each ball was twice as meaningful as the last.

Serious backgammon players employ the doubling cube. This is a die with a different number on each face; you can turn it so that the topmost face expresses the number of times the initial stake has been multiplied. Each over was like the constant resetting of this cube: 2, 4, 8, 16, 32. Then the last ball of the over, the 64 ball, damned if you'll get me with this one: and it's quicker, it's hit an irregularity in the pitch, it's hopped belly-high but I'm behind it, I'm playing it, I'm playing it *down* and the man at silly point is diving at my feet at a ball that's already bounced.

As we moved towards the end the proceedings assumed an air of serene inevitability. It was as if our opponents accepted this too. Marcus took the last over, celebrating the last ball – he had been counting – with an overacted swipe. Victoria and Albert Museum 240 for four declared, Tewin Irregulars 81 for eight. Match drawn.

Our opponents, though frustrated, understood. At least to a degree. Sure, we could have swiped and biffed, got out and lost, but we chose to make our opponents earn their victory. And they fell short. Fell short after an enthralling hour or so of sport. Such lopsided encounters have their meaning in all sports, but perhaps especially in cricket, a sport in which you can fail to win but still taste the glorious bloody-minded pleasures of not bloody well losing.

It was a match that summed up my time with the Irregulars. I had never really got topsides of cricket but, on the other hand, I hadn't been defeated. Match drawn.

I had made my tryst with cricket long, long after those childhood daydreams of glory. For a good many seasons I was, indeed, a cricketer. I belonged. I had a white cable-knit jumper. I had shoes with spikes that made a wonderful noise when I walked over concrete. I had batted and bowled and caught: I had been bowled, I had missed, I had dropped. I am one of the endless numbers of cricketers who, across the years, agreed to put themselves to the manifold tests of the sport, and who, in one way and another and after a fashion, had taken them on and passed.

And been forgotten.

Everyone who ever played any sport has sharp memories of those rare daydream moments of triumph, moments in which it sometimes seems that the individual blades of grass can be recalled one by one. These are set off in sharp relief against those dark experiences of failure, sport's Island where Dreams come true, the times when sport tells you without compromise that you are less of a person that you hoped. These things are shared by everyone who ever tried to play any sport ever invented: but perhaps the duffer has the advantage here because the great moments are so rare, the disappointments so abject. And it's the moments of greatness that remain most vivid in the memory, which is perhaps what sport is all about. In retirement we're all great players: not because we blind ourselves to our failures but because it's the good sporting memories that refuse to die. So I, too, was a champion.

Disappointment and humiliation are an ineluctable part of the sporting experience, but we can all set these things off against the other kind of memory: those times when sport seems to take us beyond joy and offer moments – however brief, however illusory – in which we seem to glimpse the endless vistas of eternity.

But come. The match is ended: go forth in peace. The pub awaits. Nicky's generous-hearted congratulations. Handshakes of the bowlers who failed to dismiss us, the silly point who was unable to catch me. The sense that even our opponents were aware that they had taken part in a rare kind of drama and that we were all a little richer for that afternoon beneath the deer park. Marcus and I had shared something that binds us. And that none of it matters: none of it matters in the slightest, and that's the greatest glory and wonder of it all.

# Chapter 40

# Sporting Perfection

It was folly and misfortune that drove me to greatness. Not greatness as the world sees it: but it was unquestionably the finest sporting performance of my life, absolutely the best I was capable of – and if that's not great I'd like to know what is. It's the sort of greatness that lies within us all, it links us with the greatest sporting performers of history, and it's precisely – but *precisely* – what sport can give to every one of us.

When you travelled to a show in Jan's lorry you tended to arrive late. After all, she had a yard to run, and as one of life's great optimists she tended to think that time was more generous and forgiving than it is and that it would all work out for the best in the end. That day at Potton it did. At least for me.

It was a cross-country event: my task was to ride a few miles over a course of jumps, fastest time wins. My plan that day was to compete in the smaller of the two classes on offer, the one with lower fences. The event had already started by the time we arrived so there was no opportunity to walk the course first. In other words, when I got to the start after warming up, I didn't actually know where I was going. I could see where the first fence was – it had a nice big figure 1 on it, so there was a helpful clue – and the plan was to jump and look about for Fence 2. I had jumped at Potton before, so it wasn't that crazy. I had a rough idea of where to go. But it was, as Jason would have said, not ideal.

We came unstuck in the high teens. We were going well up to this point, jumping boldly in a smooth, easy rhythm. But damned if I could see Fence 18. I had just cleared Fence 17, so it couldn't be far, but I had no idea where it was. I took a pull: we came to a halt, and I looked around with a wild surmise. And suddenly there it was, at our feet. The course demanded a sharp right turn on landing from Fence 17, and we had completely failed to execute it. So I asked Dolores to jump from a standstill. Being the wonderful animal she was, she obliged. The snag was, as we both discovered an instant later, that it was a drop-fence – the landing side being about two feet lower than the take-off side. Dolores landed like a grand piano, slam-dunking me crotch-first on to the pommel. This was seriously painful, and in the confusion my foot slipped from my left stirrup iron. Dolores picked herself up and went hammering towards the next fence – I could see it was the next fence because it bore an unambiguous 19 – with me hanging off her left-hand side.

I made three or four attempts to get my foot back into the iron but then Fence 19 was upon us and I thought, sod it. When in doubt kick on. On I kicked, then, and we made the fence and then cleared the last ten or so fences in great if not classic style, one foot in and one foot out. Quite an impressive feat of horsemanship in its way, except that a genuinely impressive horseman wouldn't have got into such a fix in the first place. We finished clear, but we had lost several aeons of time while I was farting about at Fence 18, so we finished well down the field. I was seething with a mixture of anger, frustration, lingering pain and continuing excitement. So I made rather a point of not thinking at all about anything. It was in this frame of mind that I entered the Open class: along with, I could see, about 60 others. The fences were significantly bigger, but not beyond our scope. I opted to start as early as I could, before my ardour had time to cool.

I always hated the few minutes before the start, but I absolutely loved the moment of the go. In the start box I would be full of saucy doubts and fears, but there was always that magic trick that took place the instant the starter told us to start. It was a bit like using a zoom lens very fast indeed. One moment I saw the world in a wide-angled view, all kinds of things going on all over the place, to the left, to the right, far away. Then in a single instant, the world was reduced to a single object, and that in pin-sharp focus, and the rest of the world had dissolved into mist. That sensation came – it always came – when I locked Dolores on to that first fence. It was like locking a homing missile on to its target. All I had to do was look at the fence, move my hands and shift my body weight forward and we were exploding out of the start with the first fence at our mercy. We cleared it in a great, effortless stride and even as we landed I was looking at Fence 2. The world was a corridor four miles long and one fence wide. Nothing else existed, or ever had existed. And I rode.

For the first time in my life I combined the ecstatic fearlessness of that mad day in Hong Kong with the precision I had learned in the showjumping ring. We jumped fast, we jumped bold, but we also jumped accurate.

Some fences we took at 45 degrees, jump-off style, to cut corners and save time and distance. The fences flowed beneath us with a sense of perfect inevitability: as if it had been fixed long ago that we would face such jumps and we would clear them. I remember that at one early fence I had the detachment to think 'that looks awfully big' even as I rode into it with complete commitment. It was big: Dolores, not often one for hesitation, checked herself just a fraction to make a good bascule – and then we were off again at the far side, picking up the pace again.

We came to Fence 17, committed even in the air to that turn hard right, and there was Fence 18 and this time she made nothing of it. I shifted my weight a little back – I remember feeling my weight in the stirrup iron as we landed – and it was as if there was no drop at all on the far side, and so we passed on towards 19 without breaking stride.

It came to an end too soon, far too soon, for I could have galloped forever that day. The last jump was a fallen tree: we had to take it at its highest and widest point and we did so without any let-up in speed or concentration and we were through the finish, clear as gin and high as a couple of kites.

It was perfection. As near as I would ever get to perfection in sport, anyway. We came third: a couple of bigger, faster, better horses beat us, no doubt with better riders on top. I was given a cheque for five pounds, which I believe I still have somewhere.

Tennis players talk about being 'in the zone', as if the fleeting experience of sporting perfection was a physical place. Psychologists call this state of arousal and perfection 'the flow'. It's not unique to sport, far from it, but it's most vividly witnessed and perhaps most readily experienced in sport. The French cyclist Jean Bobet called it '*la volupté*': 'delicate, intimate and ephemeral. It arrives, takes hold of you, sweeps you up and then leaves you again. It is for you alone. It is a combination of speed and ease, force and grace. It is pure happiness.'

This is quoted in Ed Caesar's excellent book about the marathon, *Two Hours: The Quest to Run the Impossible Marathon*. And he continues, talking of Geoffrey Mutai of Kenya, who ran what was then the world's fastest marathon, but alas in a race – Boston – that isn't recognised for official world records. Mutai calls this exalted state 'the Spirit'. 'The way he understood it, the brutality of his training regime – 125 fierce miles a week – was endured to attain this sensation … The Spirit has allowed Mutai the courage to remake the sport of marathon running and to destroy previous conceptions of what was possible; to lose his own fear, and implant it in the hearts of his competitors.'

That day at Potton – alone of all my sporting days – I was in the zone. I felt the flow, I experienced *la volupté*. I encountered the Spirit and I performed as well as I ever could have performed. Of all the things I ever did in sport, this was by far the greatest, and all the time I spent doing sport and mostly failing was worth it for those few minutes when the Spirit came calling and found me for once at home.

It was the last time I ever rode Dolores in competition. Things went badly amiss with her. I chose to stick with her rather than trade her in for a horse with which I could compete. She meant more to me than competition, more to me than any damn sport. I had her for 25 years, she bore two fine foals and she died aged 32 at my place in Norfolk.

This is not to downplay sport, merely to get it in perspective. A professional rider would have made another decision and I pass no judgement on that. Plenty of riders at my level would have done the same: I pass no judgement on them either. For some people competition is what horses are all about, what horses are *for*. I took another road, nor am I unique in that. It's another of those personal frontiers, the logical result of being the kind of person you happen to be.

My decision to stick with Dolores made it perfectly, almost pedantically, clear that when it came to the put-to, I was not really all that much of a sportsman.

Love does odd things to people. My love of sport was a shallow thing compared to more pressing matters.

Part Three

# Red Dwarf

A Star in Decay

# Chapter 41

# The Fall of Oedipus

I'd like to make it clear from the start that I was trying to win throughout. I never eased off. And that was the beauty of it.

For some years my half of the family would gather in numbers at my sister's place in the West Country for a few days after Christmas. There was a converted barn alongside the house, and there we used to play ping-pong. There was a lot of space, so we could let ourselves go. Most evenings we would play a doubles match. Doubles was good because (a) it included all who wanted to play, and (b) the format is a less likely source of tension than singles. We always played Barneses vs in-laws: me and my father against Roob and Salty.

It was a good match-up, the games always satisfyingly close, no team predominant. We tended to play after dinner, between champagne and Jack Daniel's, Salty being a generous host. The standard of table tennis was of a kind to be expected in such circumstances: intense, uninhibited, cheerful, sport being effortlessly capable of overcoming any apparent contradictions.

It was the last time we all gathered in this way, though we didn't know it then; changes in family circumstances required us to invent new traditions. And one evening – this time after tea and before champagne – my father and I opted for a match at singles. Him against me. Again. Or still. We normally managed one such match in the course of the stay, and I always won. I hadn't lost to my father in years. Naturally I expected to win again.

But I didn't. My father was seeing it well right from the first point: the blade-down slasher as good as it had ever been. I countered with my axeman-spare-that-tree forehand loop, but it never seemed to land on the right side of the table. I changed tactics and started to play conservatively: get the ball over the net and wait for him to balls it up. But he never did. I did. I played safe and still made mistakes: I hit long, I hit the net, I played tentative shots that sat up and begged to be slashed. He won in straight sets, and it was the last time we ever played: for the lack of a table rather than anything else.

There was something wonderfully appropriate about this. A part of me was complicit: welcoming the setback for reasons of affection, respect for time, for family, and for the natural drama of sport. I felt that I was taking part in something meaningful, even though my task was to lose. Perhaps those fine cricketers of the V&A felt something of the same thing as Marcus and I inched our way towards the sanctuary of the draw.

Sport is an unfolding story and stories have always been my job. But in a way that's true of everyone: we humans are a species of fabulists, and sport is a fabulous way of expressing that part of our being. And perhaps even when sport reaches a point of vertiginous drama at the highest level there is still a sense of duty to the narrative that haunts the participants. In that great cricket match between England and Australia at Headingly in 1981 – Botham's resurgence – I wonder: did the Australian cricketers find themselves compelled by the force of narrative to go along with the extraordinary counter-assault of Ian Botham and, the following day, to the power of Bob Willis who took them on in a trance of cricketing perfection?

I no more let the old bugger win than Australia let England win, but there seemed to be higher forces at work than those of mere ability. It just seemed right that this should happen, just as it feels right that we have had no further opportunity to take each other on. Sport creates myths: sport is nothing less than mythology in the raw. That's true for those who play and for those who watch. There are sporting myths that unite nations and the world: Headingly 1981, the World Cup Final of 1966, Jonny Wilkinson's drop-goal, Steve Redgrave's last gold medal, Jesse Owens and Hitler, Pelé (not the Lamma Island one), the Hand of God, Usain Bolt's world-record-breaking boogie: and on and on and on.

But there are also more private sporting myths, myths that unite just a few people: and in a way that's even more vivid, because it's almost a secret. The Shrug Ball, Mart not walking, the Fish in full flight, Eddy saving the day, me and Marcus saving another. Sometimes there are myths that involve just one other: and the Oedipal ping-pong series is like that. It's all about the long peace that followed historical and now almost-forgotten tensions: the fact that losing this last game was in its way as gratifying as winning it would have been 30 or 40 years earlier.

But there is another kind of sporting myth. That is the myth unshared and unshareable: part of the great personal mythology that helps us to cope with the world and our place in it. Sport can supply these in generous quantities: the last great ride at Potton, a running, tumbling catch I made when fielding at cover, a certain moment playing five-a-side football when a very good player passed rather than took a shot because he knew he couldn't beat me.

When sport is played with sincerity, at no matter what level of ability, it provides narratives and myths that unite people and myths that help to define them. So here I stand, hero of my own myth, yes, and abject villain and victim too. Some failures and some defeats are still capable of causing me pain: but not the last ping-pong match. I walked away from it oddly happy. And, besides, it was now surely time for Salty to open the champagne.

# Chapter 42

# The Big Fish Cup

Fish died of a heart attack at Edgbaston cricket ground in Birmingham, and, if there was a certain appropriateness in that, he was far, far too young. He and I were never friends away from the cricket field, but he was a great man who enriched my life. I should, then, have shown better grace about the match that was held in his memory.

Fish had left Hertfordshire for the Cotswolds, and here he captained the second XI at Moreton-in-Marsh. He was at least twice the age of every other player in the team: he mother-henned the young cricketers and showed them what the game, what all sport, is really all about, how to bowl, how to bat, how to win, how to lose. As a result of this, there was a challenge from Moreton to Tewin Irregulars: to meet and play for the Big Fish Cup.

It was by then nearly 20 years since I had last stepped on to a cricket pitch and I really didn't want to do it again. Horses occupied all that was left of my need for action. Besides, I didn't want to do appallingly what I had once done only fairly badly. I didn't want to field and, for that matter, I didn't want to bat or bowl. I was out of practice for dressing-room banter. I made every excuse to get out of it, even when it transpired that the Irregulars were to be captained by Fish's oldest son, Mark, also known on the cricket field as Fish or Fishy. It was Salty doing the organising; he and Fish were friends to the last, and he was deeply affected by his death. Inevitably he organised me against my will, and fixed up a lift from Suffolk to Moreton. So there really was no getting out of it. Thus it was that I batted and bowled in two match-winning partnerships with the finest player who ever turned out for the Irregulars.

Luke Sellers was – is – Salty's oldest child and only son. We share, then, 25 per cent of our genes. He shares 50 per cent of his genes with my sister, who had never shown any great talent at any sport, and 50 per cent with Salty, who was OK at the level the Irregulars played. This is not on the face of it a recipe for a great cricketer: but more or less since Luke was able to walk, he was able to bowl straight. He went through all the age levels at county level, was a fag paper or so away from playing first-class cricket, and these days he works in cricket professionally with high-level coaching qualifications. There is a photograph in my father's sitting room of two players walking off the pitch at Tewin Green in pads, carrying bats: my father, in his late 60s, and Luke, about ten. He was even better in his mid-20s.

Well, there was a decent turnout at Moreton and it was good to see some old friends again. It was agreed that we would play a kind of extended beer match: 30 overs each way, no player to bowl more than three. We batted first and did so adequately, but without distinction. I came in down the order, resignedly. Luke was in at the other end, and we exchanged words. Bumped gloves.

And I was batting again.

At once I felt the fierce old emotions going: no, you bastard, you're not getting me out, not this ball. Along with the old fear: please don't hurt me, please don't humiliate me.

The block I learned in those historic sessions with Eddy in the indoor nets seemed to have been hard-wired into my system. Little trigger-movement shuffle: meet the ball with the stone-dead bat. And again. And again. End of the over. Bump gloves. Watch Luke from the other end. He was a bowler who had made himself an effective smiter, and he smote to good effect. End of the over. Bump gloves. So I blocked, and then turned one on to the leg side for a single and got Luke back on strike. And so on. We had a partnership of 30-odd, of which my contribution was two.

Glove-bumping wasn't in fashion when I played. I found it a fine thing, especially as the fellow glove-bumper was my nephew and a proper cricketer and a hell of a good guy as well. For all kinds of reasons I found myself really rather happy. Fish would have approved, and made the right kind of jest.

Fielding was rather less fun. These great cricketers whose lives we envy: think how much of their lives they spend fielding. And not often with the consolation of action: you're out there doing stuff just in case the ball comes your way. I was stiff and slow: 'Come on, at least five there,' shouted a spectator – there were maybe half-a-dozen of them – as I set off in pursuit of a well-struck ball. One moment I remember though. I had been shifted out to the boundary to accommodate a player who could hit a bit: as he went up to the other end, I remember calling to our captain: 'Back on the one, Fish?' There was a sense of events turning full circle, of life continuing, of cricket being passed, not without relief, into the hands of the young.

All the same, it was rather dispiriting, because they were well above the run rate with wickets in hand, and they seemed to be taking the match away from us with some ease. But one of the great skills of captaincy in this type of game is in the way you use your big guns. You mustn't seek to bludgeon your opponents to bits if you happen to possess a superior weapon. That would spoil the match and the day. On the other hand, your best player, when called on, must play with proper sincerity. Luke was finally asked to bowl when they were six wickets down and about eight runs short of a winning total. He operated the truly devastating tactic of bowling straight. And really quite briskly, though not at full throttle. And he delivered us a double-wicket maiden.

Which was all very well, but Fish then asked me to bowl the next over. It looked as if we would lose the match because of my ineptitude. I felt distinctly unhappy as I measured out my run, all six paces of it. And sent down the first ball. A non-turning off-break, obviously. My God, it was on the money, there or thereabouts anyway. I bowled one bad ball in the over, which went for four, but I also bowled five decent balls that didn't. No yips that day, thank God. So Luke bowled another over and knocked over the last two. Almost literally.

And I felt a pleasure long dormant. Victory.

I felt a foolish euphoria as that last wicket fell, almost as if I'd done it myself. I felt an equally foolish love of my team-mates: that fleeting, footling, lovely and meaningless pleasure that victory in sport can bring. Steve Archibald, the footballer, said that team spirit was an illusion glimpsed in victory: but victory is the greater illusion: the illusion that you've conquered the world and that all problems are now at an end. Sport brings many pleasures in its path and this is by no means the least of them. Victory is, at least for a moment, the healing of all harms. And Barnes, clean-bowled for two runs with bowling figures of 1-0-4-0, had been a part of it.

Ridiculous, I know. Wonderful too: ridiculous that it's so wonderful, wonderful that it's so ridiculous.

# Chapter 43

# The Very Essence of Sport

I used to sit next to Mike Atherton at Test matches when we were both writing about cricket for *The Times*. His laptop, when at rest, showed a picture of a dashing, good-looking young lad smiting a cricket ball to the outer limits of the surrounding countryside. This was his son Josh: as you would expect, a promising young cricketer. And a keen one. Athers, a former England cricket captain and all that, is equally keen, keen to get it right as a parent. To walk the tightrope between indifference and pushiness, to be always encouraging, never demanding. So he won't badger Josh into practice, but when Josh suggests that they go to the local club for a net, Athers is always up for it. I can almost see them at their practice: a cheerful intensity leavened with running jokes, with guarded, carefully worded advice and bags of praise, characterised by the real athlete's ability to distinguish what was genuinely good from what merely looked it. The ball struck alarmingly hard, the sweet concussion of ball striking bat in exactly the manner the striker intended.

It's not like that at my place. My older boy, Joe, hated a ball from the first moment he was offered one. He would throw it unhandily into a bush and look for something interesting. I tried several times, but it was always the same. Sport has no interest for him whatsoever: I don't think he has ever watched it on television for longer than a second or two.

This is a disappointment to me in one way. Like most fathers I looked forward to sharing sport with my son, playing it, watching it, going to it. That's long ceased to matter, of course: we have shared a number of expeditions in pursuit of wildlife, and perhaps that's better – and now I must watch as he becomes entirely his own person, driven by an unstoppable urge to make music. Your children are never your own creation: this is the truth that comes to every parent as the most shattering revelation. So you walk the tightrope and do what you can to help them run their own lives and choose their own directions.

My second son, Eddie, loves sport. He sometimes watches televised sport with me, and often in the warmer months we play cricket. But it's not a lot like cricket with the Athertons. Eddie, now 14, has Down's syndrome. Our cricket, then, is bizarre by normal standards. We play in our garden in Norfolk and do so with a blue plastic cricket set.

Eddie prefers to bowl, but neither his concentration nor his coordination is entirely reliable. 'Look at the sticks, Eddie. Look at the sticks when you bowl.' Sometimes he does, and the ball floats towards me, generally dropping from eight or nine feet, and I pat it back with my best Tewin block. But quite often it goes off at 45 degrees to the intended path and one or other of us has to fetch it.

There's not much running about, because with lax muscles and ligaments Eddie gets weary pretty quickly. So the game is a series of wayward floating lobs and my attempts to reach them, sometimes with a tennis shot, usually a running forehand, sometimes with a leaping overhead block, a shot not often played in serious cricket but helpful if you want to keep the ball out of Eddie's vegetable garden. 'Well bowled, Eddie! No,

Eddie, look at the sticks. That's it! Brilliant, boy! That's the best ball you've bowled all day.' I still endeavour to play my leave shot, but these days I try and do it when the ball is going to hit the stumps rather than when it's going to miss.

Sometimes I persuade Eddie to have a bat. I was able to locate the middle of the bat with fair regularity when I bowled for the Irregulars, but it's harder to do so with Eddie at the other end. The desire to do so is for some reason inhibiting; so often I bowl tentatively and the ball hardly reaches him. But even now and then he makes contact: 'Great shot! Well played, Eddie!'

After that, if we're in the mood, we have fielding practice. Eddie can catch a ball when it's thrown nicely, and that's gratifying to us both. His next job is to hurl the ball at the stumps, now placed in front of the wall of the house, and the occasional satisfaction of sending them flying is immense: high fives all round the garden. Then it's time to stop for a drink: an apple juice for him, a beer for me, and we will sit on the bench and identify the birds that pass.

And this is the very essence of sport. That's because sport goes much deeper than mere competitiveness. Garden cricket provides us with a vocabulary of behaviour. It's a way of being together: a pattern of tasks and actions that make it possible for us to pass time together in busyness and amity.

Sport can be many things: hair-raisingly oppositional, blisteringly competitive, something to which people dedicate their lives, something that means everything, a source of beauty, power, joy, hate, love, humiliation, triumph and disaster. It's been one or two of those things for me: and that's true for everyone who has ever played a sport, for there is a spinal cord that links everyone who has ever hit a ball, thrown, kicked, leapt, run, won, lost and drawn, a cord that joins those who played at the loftiest possible level with those who played for Tewin Irregulars, a cord that links the arse-bone with the head-bone and connects everyone in sport who fits somewhere in between.

But sport begins not with the desire to win: that comes second, and sometimes a poorish second at that. Sport begins in togetherness: as a form of companionship, as a way of breathing the same air. Sport may be many other things as well, but the sporting impulse begins as a way of sharing something beautiful: a delight in movement that also involves sharing things like time, space, life. I've often mislaid that truth as I have travelled the world in pursuit of the greatest sporting events the planet can offer, but I have been reunited with that truth again and again on warm summer evenings between suppertime and bedtime.

I have known greatness, or at least the illusion of greatness. I have known horror and disaster, or at least the illusion of both. I have tested my wild hopes of glory against my personal limitations and found myself wanting. I have confronted personal inadequacy on a million occasions. I have savoured rare sweet moments of competence. I have found friendships and alliances that would have been impossible outside sport; I have cherished a loneliness still richer. I have relished a series of soul-deep (at least on my side) partnerships with a creature of a different species. I have experienced physical pain, including four concussions, one from a cricket ball and three from unplanned descents from a horse. I have known fear, a lot of that. I have on occasions revelled in such courage – or the illusion of courage – as I am capable of summoning up. I have known anger and resentment, resignation and acceptance. I have been mastered many times, and yet at times I have been the master, if only briefly. I have experienced deep humiliation. I have been blamed, I have been forgiven, and I have occasionally been praised. I have experienced, it sometimes seems, practically everything that life is capable of offering. Sport means everything to me, or so it has often seemed, at least at the time, but only because it means nothing. Playing sport is the ultimately trivial pursuit: and one that has enriched my life beyond measure. Sport matters profoundly. But only because it doesn't matter at all.

A bird flies past.

'Heron!' says Eddie. Correctly.

'Your batting was brilliant today, Eddie.'

'Yes, Dad.' He knows. He's full of quiet joy.

Sport can do that sort of thing to people.

# Acknowledgements

I am aware that some great performers in sport have a different view, but sport is actually about other people. Here are some of the people who made my sporting life possible. Many thanks to them all, and many more (plus apologies) to those I've missed out.

My father, dining-room ping-pong champion.

John Murtagh, for the great adventure of Streatham Common.

Mr Gray of Sunnyhill School.

Mr Chapman at the Cubs.

Mr Cooper at Emanuel School.

Stuart and Ian and the other rogue footballers at Emanuel.

Brian and Dick from Colts A VIII.

John, fellow-skiver.

Gill at Dragon Hall, my first riding teacher, who taught me to fly. Also Nita and Chris for a thousand kindnesses. In memory of Helen and Carrie.

Pete, John the Farmer and Ant from Gwai-Loong.

Tim, Chris, Robert, Jeremy, the Finches and many others from Tewin Irregulars. In memory of Paul the Fish, Eddy and David.

Jan's Place: Jan, who else? Also Maria, Karen and everyone else who travelled in the lorry.

Finally to Eddie, garden cricketer, who showed me what sport is really all about.

On the book side, thanks to Charlotte Atyeo and Holly Jarrald at Bloomsbury, and as always, to Georgina Capel.